T0077672

Advance praise for

Save Your Inner Tortoise

Emotional learning has been culturally abandoned for a long time, particularly since we made reason the only source of human learning and knowledge.

Today we are collectively realizing the huge cost that that abandonment has had for all of us and the urgent need to recover that essential part of our education. Carol Courcy's book is a marvelous contribution in that direction. It clearly shows her many years of masterful coaching.

Her book is full of insight, reflection, and practices to bring back our emotional learning. She plays constantly with her humorous realism and her exquisite capacity to dream.

I recommend this book to anyone concerned with his or her emotional apprenticeship, and particularly to the coaching community to enhance their ability to bring this ability into their professional activities.

Julio Olalla, MCC
Author of *From Knowledge to Wisdom*
Founder of The Newfield Network
www.newfieldnetwork.com

Master Coach Carol Courcy delivers ways to truly be in control of your life. Her revelations of her personal discoveries coupled with insights from those who have used her approach demonstrate the power of the simple yet potent exercises. With much compassion Courcy takes you gently by the hand, showing you how to create joy and contentment in your life! I LOVE it! This is truly a primer of how to live for all of us, but especially for driven, compulsive achievers.

Joan C. King, PhD, MCC
Author of *A Life on Purpose: Wisdom at Work* and the *Cellular Wisdom* series
www.cellular-wisdom.com

The idea of developing emotional agility is very powerful and truly needed in today's dynamic times. Embracing the tortoise as a symbol of how to approach developing your emotional strength really adds the lightness that a difficult-to-discuss topic like emotions requires. *Save Your Inner Tortoise* shares solid step-by-step tools and includes great activities and exercises that showcase alternative life strategies sure to help tame the self-sacrificing, never-enough, overachiever in you.

Jane R. Flagello, EdD
Author of *The Savvy Manager: 5 Skills that Drive Optimal Performance*
www.thesavvymanager.biz

Carol Courcy is simply amazing. She was my guide to a new realm of awareness and possibility in her Emotional Agility course. Her two questions "What do you want instead?" and "What emotion would serve you in getting there?" shifted my perspective about emotions forever. Rather than being at the mercy of external events or my unconscious habits and ways of being, I realized that I was in the driver's seat of my emotions—and my experiences. I learned ways to shift my emotions on purpose and develop practices that continue to give me access to more confidence, fulfillment and joy. What I learned continues to inspire and inform my life and work.

Angela Stauder
www.thrivagility.com

SAVE
YOUR INNER
TORTOISE!

**LEARN HOW TO CROSS THE FINISH LINE
JOYFUL AND SATISFIED**

CAROL COURCY

BALBOA.
PRESS

A DIVISION OF HAY HOUSE

Copyright © 2012 Carol Courcy

All rights reserved. No part of this book may be used or reproduced by any means, graphic, electronic, or mechanical, including photocopying, recording, taping or by any information storage retrieval system without the written permission of the publisher except in the case of brief quotations embodied in critical articles and reviews.

Balboa Press books may be ordered through booksellers or by contacting:

Balboa Press
A Division of Hay House
1663 Liberty Drive
Bloomington, IN 47403
www.balboapress.com
1-(877) 407-4847

Because of the dynamic nature of the Internet, any web addresses or links contained in this book may have changed since publication and may no longer be valid. The views expressed in this work are solely those of the author and do not necessarily reflect the views of the publisher, and the publisher hereby disclaims any responsibility for them.

The author of this book does not dispense medical advice or prescribe the use of any technique as a form of treatment for physical, emotional, or medical problems without the advice of a physician, either directly or indirectly. The intent of the author is only to offer information of a general nature to help you in your quest for emotional and spiritual well-being. In the event you use any of the information in this book for yourself, which is your constitutional right, the author and the publisher assume no responsibility for your actions.

Printed in the United States of America

ISBN: 978-1-4525-3905-8 (sc)
ISBN: 978-1-4525-3904-1 (e)
Library of Congress Control Number: 2011919164

Balboa Press rev. date: 2/24/2012

To Paul

THE best hubby this woman could have

CONTENTS

PREFACE

Calling all fellow self-sacrificing "never enough" overachievers! Helmet a bit too dented? Too big a rocket on your back? Need a good rest? Want to retire from this life strategy? Me too. I began my retirement about 15 years ago.

In the mid-1990s, like many fellow self-sacrificing never-enough overachievers, I was driven in life. I pushed and pulled hard to give what I thought others wanted or needed. On the surface I looked successful—if not a bit tired or harried. If honest with myself, I thought I was damaged goods or flawed in some profound way. I didn't think I was overachieving at all. Despite compliments, promotions, bonuses, kudos, and positive assessments of me and the work I completed, whatever I did wasn't ever enough. I never quite measured up. I could always find someone else to compare myself to unfavorably. My ever-striving sensibilities had me always coming up short in life. There was always something more I could have done. Should have done. Any attempt at satisfaction or pride was trounced by my internal "itty bitty bitchy committee" hollering about what more I needed to do or should have done. Mind you, on the outside I talked a good professional game. I smiled a lot, thanked people for appreciating my work, and accepted their congratulations graciously. However, on the inside, the "never enough" flourished. Few knew of my personal worries about measuring up.

As a coach and lifelong learner, the approach I now take is one of increasing well-being rather than fixing something that is wrong with me, my clients, or their organizations.

My turning point in 1994 was Martin Seligman's *Learned Optimism* that turned me toward finding ways to increase well-being. He offers:

> *I have learned that it is not always easy to know*
> *if you are a pessimist and that far more people*
> *than realize it are living in this shadow.*
>
> *A pessimistic attitude may seem so deeply rooted as to*
> *be permanent. I have found, however, the pessimism is*
> *escapable. Pessimists can in fact learn to be optimists.*
> ~ Martin Seligman

My "never ever quite enough" did indeed have a pessimistic shadow. I was pessimistic about my talents. That fed my fear of never measuring up and heightened my awful-izing (worrying) about my future. I had to please my customers and boss or else I'd never get work again. Seemed like a never-ending ride on a gerbil wheel.

I had an *aha* moment thanks to Seligman. Simply calling it pessimism and considering I could learn optimism fired up hope that I could indeed leave the shadows of my personal flaws for more lightness of spirit toward myself and more feelings of happiness and fulfillment.

Although insightful, I was left wondering exactly HOW one does that. I was hungry for more. I read other books on emotions by Daniel Goleman, the Dalai Lama, Candace Pert, and Paul Ekman. Great information and insights there too. However, the path to how to live in more desirable emotions wasn't yet obvious to me.

I wanted an owner's manual with instructions.

Another fortunate turn came during my second ontological coach training program. Although already a Certified Coach, I wanted to be a credentialed Master Certified Coach. (Of course I'd do a second course and get a higher credential. I am after all an overachiever—one is not enough.) I posed the "how do I leave my pessimism?" question to my Mentor Coach Jan Goldman, PsyD, whom I considered a masterful teacher and coach. Gratefully she took my question seriously, and through working with her I opted to pursue what turned out to be two life-changing strategies. In our early meetings, I discovered a pattern of never staying with a thing long enough to become masterful at it. I was a "jumper." Easily bored after the first sets of challenges were successfully completed, I would switch. (I went from retail to ski instructor, to high school teacher, back to retail—this time in management—to consulting and training, entrepreneur business owner, executive, etc., etc., etc.)

Jan offered that without an ability to deeply feel satisfaction, I would continue to be driven to always do more and be better than expected, resulting in a habit of overextending, worry, and exhausting hours at work. I was driving myself somewhere fast without declaring my purpose or conditions of satisfaction. BIG MISTAKE.

What dramatically changed that life pattern were two of Jan's coaching "homework" assignments: 1) Learn the emotion of satisfaction and 2) think of a question that I would enjoy researching for at least ten years. (Ten years? Was she kidding? What kind of question could possibly hold my interest for ten years? Didn't she remember I was a "jumper"?)

I am usually a quick study. However, much to my surprise as a 40-year practitioner of "never ever enough," I found a simple emotion of satisfaction perplexing to learn. As usual, my second-guessing habit engaged full throttle. *Isn't satisfaction akin to laziness? Won't contentment cancel out all my ambitions for promotions, bonuses, better jobs, better bosses, more clients, or better companies? This is the wrong coaching assignment. In fact, isn't satisfaction un-American, undermining our economic system?* Fortunately for me, my coach did not buy into my justifications.

As it turns out, satisfaction was the best of emotions for me to learn and practice. The same is true for others wanting to exit their excessive self-sacrificing, never-enough, overachieving ways. Remember, tortoises don't jump—they consider and change course.

Being an "ever striving" person, having no satisfaction as a counterbalance was a surefire route to exhaustion and disillusionment: anger for my staying too long at a company or in a relationship; regrets for not staying long enough in a good situation, and my pattern of unreasonable guilt for not doing more. Over time I developed a good case of long-standing resentment that I was STILL not happy after all that work.

Fairly early into the assignment I discovered I actually liked satisfaction. My days, although busy, felt less pressured now that I had an "enough" point. I started to leave the office on time, pleased with my day's efforts. I felt a new sense of freedom. Free to say yes or no to projects. Love for my work reappeared. My fears of laziness never materialized. My ambition had some boundaries. My tendency to overcommit lessened with practice. The promotions, bonuses, and kudos kept coming. I simply worked fewer hours. With more time on my hands, I had space to think about the meaning I wanted for my life. Gratitude began to appear on a regular basis. I got a glimpse of joy and found it tantalizing.

I was on to something here. Those realizations launched me toward my ten-year research question:

Can we really (and I do mean REALLY) spend more time in the emotions we prefer than in the ones we dislike?

I had spent a lot of time in dislike, worry, feeling coerced to be better. Could I undo long-term patterns? Could I support others in doing the same?

Turns out, yes—a resounding and profoundly gratifying yes.

That original proposition started in 1994 and thankfully continues to this day. As I learned satisfaction and dozens of other positive emotional attitudes along the way, my curiosity also expanded to new questions:

- Can we bring back an emotion? *I like how I was last week!*
- Can we lessen an emotion's hold or effect? *I am sick and tired of feeling this way.*
- How do we extend and strengthen an emotion? *I want more of this in my life.*

And thus my passion for understanding and teaching what I call "emotional agility" was born. To my profound satisfaction and joy, you are reading the result: a book of simple practices that will help you create new emotional habits that encourage your version of satisfaction and joy.

MY STYLE AND COACHING CREDENTIALS

I profoundly respect how busy you are and how oppressive ONE MORE TASK can feel. However, I also have enough irreverence, humor, and stamina to stick with you as you move from what doesn't work to what does. My goal is to help you reduce what is on your plate, to remain responsive while increasing satisfaction and enjoyment. Ultimately, I want you to trust yourself to do the necessary work. Do this work at your own speed. Use what works. Set aside what you are not ready for. Give the learning a good chance to work. Toss what doesn't work for you.

I also recognize that credentials are important for initiating trust in me and the learning path I propose. In addition to my personal expertise gained through my own learning, I have spent more than 5,000 hours coaching managers, supervisors, executives, students, and clients in the U.S., Canada, Mexico, Europe, and parts of Asia. Having been a vice president for two organizations over a span of 12 years, I have an appreciation for the conundrums experienced by leaders whose well-being can take a hit in today's high-performance business environment, where overdoing is a norm or badge of honor.

Coaching Credentials

- International Coach Federation Master Certified Coach (MCC) since 2000
- Member Newfield Network and ICF credentialing teams since 2001
- Board Member ACTO (Association for Coach Training Organizations) 5 years
- Newfield Certified Ontological Coach (NCOC™) 1996
- Newfield Certified Coach (NCC™) 1994
- Action Technologies Certified Ontological Coach 1990

Assessment Tool Certifications and Professional Designations

- MBTI (Myers-Briggs Type Indicator)
- Personal Directions and V-CAS (360° instruments)
- Talent Builder™; Career Focus™; Career Resiliency©
- Workflow Analysis for Business©

MIGHT YOU BE A MEMBER OF THE SELF-SACRIFICING, NEVER-ENOUGH, OVERACHIEVING CLUB?

If you picked out this book, chances are you are familiar with some aspects of life inside the gerbil wheel. Following is a list of typical behaviors of our crowd. CHECK ALL THAT APPLY.

- ❏ You care deeply about the work you do, the well-being of your family, co-workers, employees or community—or all of the above—yet often feel exhausted, alone, underappreciated, or overwhelmed.
- ❏ Do you always want more from life? (*I should... I need to... I must...*) (Money, time, being thinner, heavier, healthier, higher up in your organization, more respected, better liked, etc.?) Has this urge for more, better, sooner, or easier gone too far?
- ❏ Do you know what *enough* is or looks like? Can you stop before your body says no more? (What exactly is enough money? Enough work on this project? Enough for today? What date is soon enough?) Can you leave a task, or a day, in peace?
- ❏ When you meet a goal or keep a commitment, do you always see more to do or a better way you could/should have done it? (Recognize overdoing perfectionism?)
- ❏ Does your pleasing others have boundaries? (What is enough pleasing?)
- ❏ Do you only focus on mistakes or failures? Is there no pleasing you? (When you receive positive feedback, do you look for what you did wrong or what was not up to standard first?) Is the highest possible mark or score the ONLY valid score for you?
- ❏ When you compare yourself to others, do you ever measure up?

❑ With your own successes, do you stop to feel and enjoy the satisfaction? A deep sense of joy? Or do you bypass that part? (*Can't rest on my laurels. I'll be left out if I don't keep up.*)

❑ Can you receive a compliment or a genuine "thank you" without dismissing it or diminishing yourself? (*Oh, that's okay. It wasn't a big deal.* And it was. *I don't deserve ...*)

❑ Do you crave acknowledgment, gratitude, or praise, yet feel a bit uncomfortable when you get it?

❑ Does your organization foster this *never-enough* attitude? (Do you as a leader foster the same? What is enough from employees? Is *enough* a dirty word, or not good business?)

❑ Do you say yes when you mean no? Do you say yes and then break your promises to others to keep another commitment? (To children, your spouse, colleagues, etc.)

❑ Do you easily forgo promises to yourself? Do you automatically accommodate others and put yourself last? Do you ever get to you?

❑ You have *very* good reasons and excuses for overextending. Do you pride yourself in how much work you take on? Does a "better than" or "I know more than" appear? (*Just a little longer. Who else will? No one but me could ... They need me here.*)

❑ Might you be overdoing on self-sufficiency? (Remember the tortoise on the cover? Is your helmet dented with "blows from life"? (*I'm OK. I don't need help. I have to do this on my own. It's easier if I do it myself.*)

❑ Does your self-sufficiency spread to others? Might you be "saving" people who haven't asked to be saved?

❑ Do you resist or avoid asking for help? (*I haven't ever asked, but I am sure there is no one to help. Needing help is a sign of weakness or lack of intelligence. I am the only one who cares or can do this.*)

❑ Add your own…

_____

_____

_____

_____

_____

_____

Carol's Coaching Corner: Did you check too many boxes for your taste? Did your own version of "not enough" fire up again?

CONGRATULATIONS! It shows you are aware of what you do and how you go about doing it.

If you're going to succeed in using this book, awareness of who you are and tend to be these days is a critical step. _Later you will see that these insights are the very tools you'll use to enact change._

INTRODUCTION

As the book cover suggests, my ideal reader is the self-sacrificing, never-enough overachiever who, in some fashion, is overdoing in life. In this crowded international group, often missing are recurring and extended feelings of satisfaction and joy. More likely to be present are anxiety, fretting, frustration, and other aspects of fear. Also common is accommodating and accepting these stress-generating emotions.

Many in this group can relate to the picture on the front and back covers. We sometimes need a helmet to protect ourselves when we've strapped a rocket to our backs to push through life. Even though we KNOW we are overwhelmed from saying yes too much, and might even be angry at our situation in life, we sometimes put on an even BIGGER rocket to cross our finish lines.

Take a moment. Sit back and take a couple of deep breaths.

What happens these days after you cross your finish lines?

- Is it worth it?
- Did you stop and enjoy the fruits of your efforts? Or is there NO STOPPING?

Keep breathing.

- Instead of experiencing genuine satisfaction and joy, do you find yourself with still MORE to do? *Who has time to rest? Who else but me will get this done right?*
- Have you been ignoring a nagging "should" from your inner wisdom that says something needs to change, and soon?

- Is your helmet full of dents from failing to take care of yourself or other postponements?
- Are you feeling disillusioned, plagued by guilt, or feeling the onset of regret and sadness?
- Might a smaller rocket (or no rocket at all) be a better life strategy?
- Is joy so far away that it seems impossible?

I personally think it a shame that well-intentioned, caring people are too busy and postpone feeling joy. My mission in life is to add some balancing weight of pleasure on the overweighted scales of never enough.

WHY THE TORTOISE?

I laughed when I first saw the picture of the tortoise with the helmet and the rocket strapped to its back. It so fit with how I sometimes lead my own life. I have felt a bit beaten up by life and need some protection, as the helmet suggests. It was the rocket strapped to the back of the tortoise that compelled me to use this image for the covers. Those of us who push and pull our way through life need boosters to get ourselves through our many tasks and responsibilities. (Caffeine, sugar, long workdays, working on weekends and during vacations.) I thought many of my readers would also find it humorous and fitting.

It also reminded me of Aesop's fable about the race between the tortoise and the hare. The story, as you probably recall, is about a hare who ridicules a slow-moving tortoise. Surprisingly, the tortoise challenges the hare to a race. When the race starts, the hare speeds off, leaving the tortoise far behind. Confident of winning, the hare decides to take a nap midway through the race. However, when it awakes, the hare finds the tortoise crawling slowly but steadily across the finish line.

Like the hare, we self-sacrificing, never-enough overachievers assume that at our hectic pace we can cross our ever-increasing number of finish lines. As with the hare, sometimes we find out too late we used the wrong strategy.

Maybe now is a good time to SAVE YOUR INNER TORTOISE. This is an ideal book when more of the same in your life is NOT an option. Ideal in that I know what that is like. I have found effective ways, for myself and hundreds of clients, to undermine undesirable patterns.

My aim is to make your journey across your finish lines simple and effective—right from the beginning. If you bring genuine interest, you can leave the what and how to me.

I have designed and will present *Four Steps for Saving Your Inner Tortoise.*

By means of these four steps, this book introduces insights and instructions for alternative life strategies to help you to cross your finish lines with increased satisfaction. Plus, if you are so inclined, learn how to make regular and extended visits to peace of mind and joy. This book is full of awareness activities and simple practices to help you recover your wise inner tortoise. Along the way you will hear fascinating quotes from favorite authors and teachers, insights from students and clients, as well as my story of my own journey from resentment to contentment.

Step 1: Get to know your inner tortoise.

Experience insightful activities through which you get a clear picture of where you are overdoing while underdoing well-being.

Step 2: Give your self-sacrificing, never-enough, overachieving tortoise a break.

Interrupt your current life patterns to create an essential open space for new learning to take hold.

Step 3: Save your inner tortoise ... and cross finish lines joyful and satisfied.

You don't have to change everything for everything to change. Introducing the *Universal Emotions of Well-being.*

Step 4: Create and cross new finish lines.

Use what you've learned to design and implement your own ideas for extending your well-being for longer periods, or to other relationships and areas of responsibility.

GOOD TO KNOW
BEFORE YOU BEGIN

I missed the Emotions 101 classes in school. No surprise. There weren't any. Our emotional smarts came from personal experiences and lessons taught by influential people like our parents, siblings, grandparents, relatives, mentors, and teachers. We are grateful for some of these lessons, and others not so much or not at all. Some experiences triggered our most basic and oldest responses of fight, flight, or freeze. You might notice that these are all related to the emotion of fear. In my own case, my preferred ways of getting through life were pleasing (fear of being disliked) and pretending I knew something when I didn't (fear of not being good enough). I was familiar with play, fun, and laughter, and then also fraught with anxiety and worry. Frankly, it was a bit confusing. I was greatly relieved to find a way out of the confusion.

Author's Story... As with my predisposition to pessimism, mentioned in my earlier story, I was also blind to the resentment that was a driving force in my life. Unbeknownst to me, you could find me whining daily about how bad off or unhappy I was in life. As with pessimism, I felt the emotion, but I did not call it out as an emotion. In a way, the emotion had me.

In October 1994, my life took its second important emotional change in direction. I discovered that beyond my pessimism, I was a resentful person too. Not cool. I considered myself a good girl, and resentment was certainly NOT something I would have admitted to. One day, as

5

part of my coach training with my mentor coach, my fellow students and I drew workshop topics out of a hat for our presentation the next day. Much to my chagrin, the paper I picked up read "resentment." I muttered to myself, *Well … you can't expect me to speak on something I know nothing about! This isn't fair.* So as to not draw attention to my problem, I quietly offered to trade with my co-facilitator, who had drawn "resignation." As a "pleaser" familiar with doing too much for others and feeling disappointment with the results, I felt resignation was an acceptable emotion for someone always trying to be a good girl. He declined. I muttered, *What? You can't do that!* He responded, "In my experience, Carol, resignation and resentment are related—like a brother and sister. Are you sure you know nothing of resentment from personal experience?" More silent muttering. *Damn him anyway! It's his fault I'll look stupid for my presentation.*

Back in my hotel room, something about what he said rang true. However, I immediately discounted that thought and returned to criticizing him, this stupid coach training course, his question, what a lousy co-presenter he was going to be, etc. *How dare he make me look bad? I might not pass this exam because of him!* I began frantically preparing while frustrated by my plight.

Around 10 p.m., FLASH! Oh, S—T (expletive)! I recognized my resentment toward my presentation partner for "making me" speak on this topic. Then another FLASH! The last eight months with my boss had been full of resentment. As the business owner, he was changing his strategic plan, and if I didn't change with him—which I didn't want to do—I would be out of work. *How dare he take my career and livelihood away from me? He should take care of my future ANYWAY. I deserve better. How could he do this to me? After all, I had worked so hard for him for the last five years. He owed me.*

My realization about my pattern of resentment was formulating clearly now: *Poor me!* and *Why me?* and whining to others had dominated my time for months. Yet another FLASH! Everyone but my boss knew my thoughts and feelings. Around him I made no complaints, no requests—just quiet seething. *Any good boss should have guessed what I was feeling and thinking. Any decent person would have guessed my feelings.* My face flushed and my heart pounded as my pent-up anger, resentment, and bitterness arose. And then … the final FLASH came around midnight.

YIKES! I really am behaving as a resentful person. In fact, I am a textbook resenter: full of expectations, yet NO complaints or requests for action to someone who could resolve my concerns. No conversation with my boss. I just expected what I *never* asked for! Surprisingly, instead of my normal defensiveness, I felt relief. I could b-r-e-a-t-h-e. At that moment, the pattern was revealed and the opening for change appeared. No wonder nothing was resolved with my boss. The one person who could do something about my situation did not know what I was feeling or thinking. I had forced him into guessing why I was grumpy with him. In my head, I had had the missing conversation many times. In reality, I had not.

The topic "I didn't know anything about" had come alive for me. My natural pessimism + my pleasing ways = active resentment. My presentation the next day began with "Hello, my name is Carol Courcy. As of 2 a.m. this morning, I am a recovering resenter." The audience's laughter and recognition of their own version throughout my talk remains a priceless memory. I was leaving my path of resentment for one of satisfaction and joy.

Carol's Coaching Corner: For some readers, it was obvious I was resentful after a few sentences. It was not obvious to me until I had a name for my pattern, and then all of a sudden I saw the pattern in many relationships and situations. The same will most likely be true with your journey. Emotions blind us in a way. They color and in some cases pollute the air we breathe, what we say and do not say, what we see and do not see. I didn't know the air I was breathing was tainted with resentment and anger. I was just breathing it.

After reading my story, you might notice some places in your own life where disappointment, anger, resentment, or feeling an unfulfilled sense of entitlement are a part of your emotional experiences. Perhaps you also notice that whining, wishing, and hoping do little to change your circumstances, results, or the relationships you want to improve.

I offer that if you want more satisfying and happier outcomes, you'll want to update your emotional habits. Perhaps, as I was "breathing" my pessimism and resentment, you too have been breathing the same emotional attitudes as always while expecting different results for yourself and from other people. You could have a long wait on your hands. Or...

Perhaps it is time to learn more about the indispensable skill of emotional learning.

WELCOME TO MY VERSION OF EMOTIONS 101

WHY EMOTIONAL LEARNING MATTERS

Emotions determine the quality of our lives. They occur in every relationship we care about—in the workplace, in our friendships, in dealings with family members, and in our most intimate relationships. They can save our lives, but they can also cause real damage.[1]

Author's Story... The preceding statement from *Emotions Revealed* by Dr. Paul Ekman was a wake-up call. In my case, "saving my life" fit my desire to leave my resenting ways. The *aha* moment at my conference was not enough to change my behavior. Back at work, I found the resentment and anger rising again. I knew I needed to have a conversation with my boss. Turns out, I didn't know how. I had some learning to do.

Some of the necessary learning came from the authors of *A General Theory of Love*:

> The superficial purposes of emotionality are plain. Exhilaration, longing, grief, loyalty, fury, love—they are the opalescent pigments that fill our lives with vibrancy and meaning. And emotions do more than color our sensory world: they are at the root of everything we do, the unquenchable origin of every act more complicated than a reflex. [2]

Author's Story... "... at the root of everything we do!" That one phrase helped me make a connection between my resentment and my discounting the possibility of having a good conversation about my future with my boss. I can still see the look of confusion on his face when I failed to take the partnership offer after complaining to him how unhappy I was.

It dawned on me that I wanted to be *right* about how unhappy I was more than I wanted to do something that might *make me happy*. That was my first glimpse of my "unhappy-at-all-costs" habit. Although I said I wanted to be happy, I wasn't, as we say here in the U.S., "walking my talk." Later, I would see it as part of my "nothing is ever enough" pattern.

If, beyond reflexes, emotions influence how we behave in certain situations or with certain people, emotional learning opens a whole new territory of effective action. When we learn new emotions, new experiences are available. If our day-to-day emotions are affecting the quality of our lives, learning more useful or even pleasant ones might feed our practical sensibilities for feeling more rested and replenished. It's possible to learn alternatives to pessimism, anger, frustration, disappointment, sadness, and resentment.

Carol's Coaching Corner: There are hundreds of books on emotions and the new brain science that is making emotional learning more available to those interested in making important changes in their lives. I do not pretend to be anywhere near an expert on the science behind emotional learning. Here I offer a set of what I consider essential insights and provocative science from experts in their fields to help you trust yourself with the activities and practices in this book.

EMOTIONS ARE UNIVERSAL

Dr. Paul Ekman's extensive research in *Emotions Revealed* found seven universal emotional expressions: anger, sadness, fear, surprise, disgust, contempt, and happiness. His findings show that whether you are in New Guinea or New York, the facial expressions and recognition between people are the same.

Author's Story... When reading about these "behavioral essences" I found myself grateful that my own negative emotions were *not* individual character flaws, but simply a part of being human. I am even more grateful for the idea that being emotional is a part of being normal.

I noticed I was expressing a very limited set of these universal emotions. My emotional habit pattern included mostly anger, fear, and contempt (yet another aspect of resentment). I noticed a lack of surprise and especially of happiness. I wondered, if these were universal, how could I activate them in myself? Could I diminish the ones I was overdoing?

Looking at emotions as normal and seeing their patterns will be one of your strategic advantages for changing. You will see later in this book how you can determine when you are overdoing or underdoing a particular emotion. If you decide to change the pattern, you will be rewarded with plenty of activities, simple practices, and inspiring ideas from others who have preceded you.

WE CONFUSE BEING EMOTIONAL WITH BEING OVERLY EMOTIONAL

Some of our discomfort with admitting we have emotions, and our frequent avoidance of certain emotions, comes about because we confuse having normal emotional reactions with being overly emotional. We all have had experiences when we over- or underreacted. Feeling anxiety or even dread in anticipation of an important event, speech, meeting, or get-together is normal—often only to find our fears unfounded after a successful event. After a really bad day, we find ourselves joyful and excited as we see the taxi with our good friends arriving for a visit. Later, the bad day doesn't seem too bad at all. Having any number of emotions each day is natural. When getting married, we experience a confusing mix of happiness and anxiety, joy and fear. All appropriate if one accepts that all emotions are valid and a part of the human experience.

One of the skills you will develop from the activities in this book is learning to adjust your emotions. You will learn to interrupt undesirable emotions, as well as enlivening emotions you prefer. Over time you will find yourself over- or underreacting less and less, and feel a sense of increased well-being.

How can that happen?

THE SECRET TO SAVING YOUR INNER TORTOISE: EMOTIONAL AGILITY

Discovering a greater sense of well-being does NOT require more time, a new job, a different boss, or a bigger bank balance. To take a break from worry or suffering, you do not need a better past, or different family members or relationships. I present ... emotional agility. Without changing your current life circumstances, you can enter new emotional patterns and exit old ones, feel replenished, and find renewed energy.

You don't have to change everything for everything to change

WHAT IS EMOTIONAL AGILITY?

Emotion: The origin of the word emotion is *émouvoir*, "to set in motion." What are you putting in motion emotionally these days? Are you calming, stirring up, disturbing, holding tenderly, or …?

Agility is ease of movement and liveliness. For example, the ability to change the body's position efficiently requires the integration and coordination of isolated movements. As we learn a new dance move or software program, with practice we can become more and more agile and competent. So too with emotional learning.

Emotional agility: The ability to enter and exit emotions with skill, ease, and intentionality. Emotions that seem foreign to us or uncomfortable in the beginning become easier to access, as we activate them enough over time that they become part of our emotional repertoire.

Another way of looking at emotional agility is measuring your current level of agility. How agile, lively, and flexible are you? Members of the self-sacrificing, never-enough, overachieving crowd often push and pull at life. We frequently overextend ourselves for others, tolerate pain, or ignore health warnings and other signs indicating we should not do so much. Another part of our pattern? We have plenty of good reasons and excuses. We lack the agility or skill to balance all our efforts with activities that refuel us. For example, are you good at taking on challenges, yet not as good at doing what replenishes you? Do you end your days tired and satisfied with your efforts? Or just tired? Are you able to move effectively through your day-to-day commitments and then rest easy? Are you having any fun? (Or do you have to work before you play, and once your workday is over, there's no time left to bring joy to yourself or to others important to you?)

HOW DOES EMOTIONAL AGILITY WORK?

Aristotle offers a hint of the learning journey ahead:

We are what we repeatedly do.
Excellence, then, is not an action but a habit.
~ Aristotle

Think about that ... we ARE what we repeatedly do? This holds true for honorable qualities like excellence, as well as less enlivening personal patterns like exhaustion or worrying. Where might this hold true for you?

- If you repeatedly overdo or say *yes* too much, feeling overwhelmed is the natural emotion that becomes a hard habit to break. If you keep justifying your way of being, it becomes an even stronger emotional pattern.
- Saying *yes* when you mean *no* breeds resentment. Do you blame others for your yeses?
- If you repeatedly say *I cannot*, can resignation and disappointment be far behind?

Carol's Coaching Corner: Exhaustion and dissatisfaction persist with never-ending shoulds, needs, and have-tos. There is no satisfaction if there's *always* more that could or should be done. Even when done, there is more to do.

The #1 rule of those living in insufficiency and "never enough"? *Nothing is ever enough.* Little emotional agility there.

ANOTHER SECRET TO SAVING OUR INNER TORTOISE? PRACTICE!

In *Destructive Emotions*, the Dalai Lama, Daniel Goleman, and other scientists offer us advice on why emotional agility can work:

> A decade ago the dogma in neuroscience was that the brain contained all of its neurons at birth and it was unchanged by life's experiences...

> But the new watchword in brain science is "neuro-plasticity," the notion that the brain continually changes as a result of our experiences—whether through fresh connections between neurons or through the generation of utterly new neurons...

> There is an undeniable impact on the brain, mind and body from extensive practice. ... The important idea is

that this process is within reach of anyone who applies himself or herself with enough determination. ... It can be trained because the very structure of our brain can be modified. [3]

The idea of neuroplasticity combined with a yearning to accrue desirable emotional changes makes emotional agility a skill and not just a hope. We do not have to feel trapped by familiar pessimism, resentment, and a nagging sense of insufficiency. We also are not condemned to excessive pleasing, self-sacrificing, guilt, and out-of-control perfectionism forever. We do not have to wait until our circumstances in life or the people around us change. With practice, I changed. I am still changing. Hundreds of students and clients are changing. So can you.

How much and how long to practice is something you will see for yourself. By doing the activities in Steps 1 and 2, you will find ways of shifting your emotions with more ease in a surprisingly short amount of time. My strategy for this book—simple and easy. I have designed the activities and practices with quick results for you in mind. As you build skill and confidence, you will take on the more difficult situations of your choosing.

Carol's Coaching Corner: Notice the absence of *hard* or *challenging* as a standard? Instead I am using *easy* and *simple*. That is intentional on my part. As an emeritus member of the self-sacrificing, never-enough, overachiever club, I know the patterns and tendencies. Work always comes before play. And if there is no play, so be it. Hard work is seen as more valuable than easy work.

I am proposing that, for a brief period, you consider replacing the "life has to be hard in order to be valued" belief with an orientation toward satisfaction and joy as your motivating force.

You will discover that *simple* and *easy* produces results too. You have choices as to how hard you make your life.

When I am in a period of drought, my chief enemy is despair. I am afraid to harbor hope, and yet it is the gentle harboring of hope that is the antidote to dryness of the spirit. In arid times, we must practice a very gentle discipline. [4]

At every step in this book, you will learn gentle disciplines for increasing your sense of well-being. Repetition will be key to your success. Doing a bit more of what you want for yourself every day is all that is needed to increase your sense of well-being. If we combine Aristotle's and Cameron's thoughts, by practicing hope, satisfaction, joy, or playfulness we can outwit despair or other emotions we consider destructive in some way.

Carol's Coaching Corner: Replacing destructive emotional patterns with new patterns associated with well-being—such as satisfaction and joy—is a part of this learning methodology. As you engage in the activities, these new emotions influence your behavior. More well-being creeps into day-to-day life. A benefit is that you will notice what does and doesn't work in your life. (Speaking up about disappointments sooner rather than later was better for me than staying mute.) You will have a choice of doing more of what does work or going back to your old pattern. Success for you will come by doing your part.

Author's Story... Leaving my own resentment habit required me to take responsibility for my happiness. I would have to leave blaming others behind. To be honest, at the time I wasn't so sure that was something I wanted to do. I found myself hedging. After all, unhappiness wasn't so bad. *I'm really not that tired or overwhelmed.* Being unhappy didn't take much energy on my part. Blaming others was a type of relief, taking the pressure off me.

To start undoing my well-honed skills of pleasing to the point of resentment, I needed my mentor coach Jan's simple instructions on satisfaction: to say yes when I meant yes, and no when I meant no.

Although the concept seemed simple, it was not easy in all relationships. (No surprise. My boss and clients were not used to me EVER saying no. They resisted at first. One even asked me if I didn't feel well.) This initial task extended over weeks. As Julia Cameron called it, this one "gentle discipline" was more than enough to bring a newfound feeling of control over my daily work schedule. (To remain responsible for my happiness, I remain mindful of this practice to this day.)

EMOTIONAL AGILITY IN REAL LIFE

Aristotle gives us a hint about emotional agility in real life:

> Anyone can become angry—that is easy. But to be angry with the right person, to the right degree, at the right time, for the right purpose, and in the right way—this is not easy. [5]

Author's Story… Initially, I thought my recently acknowledged anger and resentment were something to get rid of. (No surprise, given that I had waited until a boiling point to express them. Who wouldn't want to stop that?) To be more realistic, my challenge was not getting *rid* of some emotions, but employing them effectively, as Aristotle suggests.

For example, over time, I found that sometimes my resentment was indeed the appropriate emotion. After someone breaks a promise, resentment or anger is appropriate, given the betrayal of trust. However, we often assume that what has been will continue to be. We live our expectations as promises to be kept forever.

What I had to practice was speaking up about my disappointments and unfulfilled expectations MUCH sooner. Although clumsy with my first few attempts, I was able to tell my boss how angry and disappointed I was that he was changing the company. In those conversations, I learned the difference between an expectation and a promise. I expected that my good work meant I had a job forever. No one had promised me that. Even I wouldn't have said that— yet I behaved as if I did. I had assumed that our good working relationship meant he would continue to want my skills. (He did!

He offered me a partnership.) When I declined, he went forward with his changes. In the end, I simply didn't like the work I would be doing. That was my choice. I had not seen it as a choice until this conversation.

After months of angst, our issues were resolved. The air felt cleaner between us. I no longer felt dread on the way to work. I had found the right moment for the conversation and the right amount of time. (A lunch, not on the run to a meeting.) I had expressed my anger to the right degree and made a complaint. Instead of damaging my relationship with further muteness, I recovered our relationship by speaking up. That had NOT been obvious to me while I was under the influence of resentment. By discovering that I could employ the emotion of anger in more effective ways, I now had a way to not leave myself or my boss wondering why our relationship was off kilter.

Emotional agility helps you recognize how your emotions are influencing your life experiences and your relationships. As Dr. Ekman suggests, emotions affect the quality of our lives. If needed, emotional agility also can show us how to have the right conversations, with the right person, for the right purpose, in the right way, at the right time, and to the right degree.

If that is good news, here is more!

EMOTIONAL AGILITY IS SOMETHING WE ALREADY KNOW

Each of us has successfully shifted an emotion or changed an attitude toward something or someone. You have probably done it this past week a few times!

Each of these is an example of emotional agility in action:

- Sighing or taking a deep breath.
- Gritting your teeth or pounding on the steering wheel.
- Telling yourself to "grin and bear it" or "make the best of something" and doing just that.

- "Sucking it up," as they say, and staying mute. (In other words, withholding a reaction.)
- Deciding to read one of those funny or inspiring emails you get that sometimes bother you, and being glad you did.
- Contacting a friend just to talk or feel better.
- Saying "enough for now" and taking a break.
- When frantic, asking for help and then feeling more at ease.
- When frantic, *not* asking for help and finding yourself more worried.
- When unhappy, intentionally doing a good thing for another and feeling your spirits lift.
- Avoiding doing something you know you will regret.
- Thinking you might regret something and doing it anyway.
- Needing a change of scenery and going to a favorite place.
- Sitting back in your chair, looking out the window for a few minutes, and then going back to work.
- Daydreaming.
- Treating yourself in a caring manner.
- Telling yourself to be nicer to someone and then doing that.
- Suspending your own desires for the sake of another.
- Being happy when you did what you said you would do—even when it was difficult.

Each of these and hundreds of other actions shifted your emotional state and, for a time, your life felt different!

Congratulations! You are *not* a rank beginner at emotional agility.

EXPECTED OUTCOMES FROM PRACTICING EMOTIONAL AGILITY

Before I invented my own ways of practicing emotional agility, my own skill was more accidental than predictable. My emotional wisdom tended to come after the fact and way too late in some situations. I kept hoping I would do better next time. Sometimes I did, but most of the time I did not. I now say that I lacked the right emotion for that situation at hand.

My aim with this book is to bring more intentionality and predictability to your developing skill of emotional agility.

As you try on new emotions in the coming days and weeks, here is what to expect:

- Less overwhelm and more relief or satisfaction
- More periods of contentment instead of ongoing frustration
- Courage or calm instead of persistent anxiety and fear
- Increased acceptance, graciousness, and dignity for yourself and others
- A vacation from persistent disappointment or regret
- Increased satisfaction instead of ever-present dissatisfaction and guilt
- Ambition instead of procrastination or inertia
- Peace instead of anger or bitterness

I hope that this section on my version of Emotions 101 has dispelled some of the mystery about having emotions. My hope is that I have triggered a desire in you to move forward with your own mastery of other approaches to a well-lived life. There is more Emotions 101 information to come, plus inspiring insights from clients and students from their journeys.

I have designed this book in an *owner's manual* format, offering dozens of insights as to *why* and *how* emotional agility works to initiate and sustain desired changes. In Steps 1 and 2, there are activities with step-by-step instructions to begin your transformation immediately. In Steps 3 and 4, as you gain confidence and skill, you will design your own learning activities for situations and relationships that you deem worthy of or necessary to change.

Ready to *save your inner tortoise*? Interested in crossing your finish lines with more joy and satisfaction?

Take a few deep breaths, and start when you are ready.

STEP 1: GET TO KNOW YOUR INNER TORTOISE

To build on Aristotle's point that "we are what we repeatedly do," one of the best ways of knowing ourselves is to observe and articulate our habits and patterns. If you go back and reread my *Author's Story* so far, you can pull out the patterns of pessimism and resentment: What did I often say? And do? What did I rarely or never say and do? If you had been in a room with me, what was the general tone of my voice? What attitude did I bring with me to life? How do you imagine my emotions influenced my day-to-day life? Which emotions were missing altogether?

You could ask similar questions while rereading the club member checklist at the end of the preface (on page xvi). Coming up in this section are a number of activities to reveal even more about your own and other club members' patterns.

Carol's Coaching Corner: Some of you might be feeling a bit anxious to "get going" or asking, "Why take this kind of time? Shouldn't we be doing something by now?"

Whoa! Have I caught you rushing or pushing? Pushing to get things off our list is one of our patterns. At this point, be wary of any rushing tendencies.

Instead of following that urge, I ask you to consider mustering some patience while exploring Step 1. *If you do what you normally do, you will get more of the same.*

TAKE A FEW DEEP BREATHS when encountering rising anxiety, negative self-assessments, or worry. The time for action will come.

HOW HAVE YOU BEEN CROSSING YOUR FINISH LINES THESE DAYS?

One of many memorable moments on my journey to a lighter way of being was finding out that a number of my emotional patterns were not of my original making. In Emotions 101 we learned about Paul Ekman's research into seven universal behavioral essences. I think of them as emotional themes that we share with our fellow human beings. We arrived on the planet with a variety of emotions. We share those emotions with every other human being on this planet.

I was not at fault for my fears and contempt. I inherited the capacity.

EMOTIONAL INHERITANCES

We may be special. We are not unique. ~ Julio Olalla

In addition to the universal essences, our habits or predisposition to be a particular way are a result of many factors. We often "see" ourselves in our family life. (How does your family celebrate holidays?) We also find patterns connected to our age. (How does your generation behave differently from an older or younger one?) Other influences on our behavior are our religious or spiritual backgrounds.

I call these "emotional inheritances." They are the stories we carry that influence the variety of emotions we feel day to day, week after week, or on particular occasions.

Author's Story... How I inherited and cultivated my ever-striving ways.

I am a middle-class, Caucasian, female, baby boomer, Roman Catholic, American. When I look carefully at the traditions of each, it seems no accident at all that I am prone to feeling inadequate and insufficient. In fact, to me it seems "never enough" is coursing through my veins. Although I do not remember electing to be this way, I am taking this opportunity to look at these parts of myself as emotional inheritances that trigger certain thinking and behavior patterns in me:

As a middle-class American, my sense of insufficiency seems natural. I am in the middle. Better off than some. Not as well off as others. The middle would be fine, except that I am bombarded with the idea that I always need something more. *You need this and that to be happy—more money, promotions, a bigger house, etc. If I don't look younger and slimmer, I will miss out. They will never hire me if I don't have more credentials.* Professionally, I have played a fine game of "never measuring up" and pushing myself to be faster, more responsive, competitive, as I moved up a ladder someone else invented.

If I didn't always want more, I was failing the American Dream.

As a Caucasian, flowing through my psyche is a perplexing combination of resignation's "not good enough," arrogance's "better than," ambition's "striving and wanting to be better," and back to resignation's "never quite making it"!

Striving and going against the grain are parts of my baby boomer generation. We hippies were against the establishment and were going to change the world. (Some are still hippies, and others are now a part of the establishment we rallied against, or somewhere in between.)

And I have my Roman Catholic faith. Who can measure up to God? With heaven in the balance, how can one NOT strive to be a good human being? Combine that with the Christian ethic that hard work is one of the measures of goodness, and we have secured a strong sense of ever striving and never being quite good enough.

In my early education, fear was a handy motivator to behave better. If I didn't get into college, I would be a failure in life. And that fear tactic was present in my professional life as well. If I didn't get promoted, I'd be left behind. If I didn't make my budget, then … If I'm not good enough, there are consequences.

Before I came across the idea of being able to change my emotions, my ever-pleasing self always put others first. Reinforcements came from family in the form of being called selfish or self-absorbed if I put myself first. (For me this was fertile ground for self-sacrifice and guilt to grow like weeds.) Factor in religious guilt for my sins, and doing more, pleasing, and being selfless seemed a pretty smart strategy. Guilt is a powerful motivator for many strivers. Overwhelm? Self-doubt? Plenty of that! One wears them as badges of honor, as we complain about how hard we work in conversations in the coffee room.

In my combination of emotional inheritances, there are also some emotions notably lacking or missing altogether. Although present, happiness and playfulness tended to be short-lived. Too many pressures to get back to work. Long-term or deep satisfaction and contentment were nowhere to be found. In my head these were akin to laziness.

My employers and clients were also on this never-enough bandwagon— you are only as good as your last deal, sale, project, or win. Growth at all costs. What have you done for us *lately*? Forty hours a week was considered part time. Overworking was an acceptable excuse for ignoring other responsibilities (family and postponing healthy practices). The thrill of success was quickly sabotaged by "I could have done more." (I remember a lovely team celebration evening with a bonus and salary bump after a year's worth of exhausting work. As I saw the $ on the check, I felt it was all worth it. The next day, "in honor of our extraordinary efforts" our team was awarded a 25 percent higher quota for the coming year. At that moment I was wondering if I could give the check back.)

> After decades of this life strategy, I was exhausted and resentful. In the end I felt I got the booby prize for all that hard work. From the perspective of emotional agility, my work and life patterns simply increased my emotional skills of anxiety, ambition, frustration, guilt, resignation, and resentment.

Missing in all of this was an answer to "What IS enough?" That is a question we will address later in this book. For now, we're focusing on discovering patterns, to see exactly how and why we get "more of the same" in life.

AWARENESS ACTIVITY
Your emotional inheritances

What have you inherited that fuels your version of self-sacrificing, never-enough overachieving? (Family traditions? Work culture? Core beliefs and values? Something else?)

_____

_____

_____

_____

_____

_____

_____

_____

_____

_____

_____

Carol's Coaching Corner: While not at fault, we are responsible for our emotions to a considerable extent. Although they are influential, we do *not* have to spend our emotional inheritances in the ways of the past. Even though we live in an ambitious environment, and although we may be predisposed to certain patterns, **we are not condemned to repeat them.**

Our human capacity for learning and taking advantage of our neural plasticity allows us to break patterns—even long-term and socially acceptable patterns.

OUR METAPHORICAL EMOTIONAL WARDROBE

As the illustration suggests, we can look at the variety of emotions we have available to us as our emotional wardrobe. Over on the right-hand side you see the rocket and dented helmet we use when pushing ourselves in life. On the left, the beach hat and fancy umbrella drink we enjoy when really relaxing or on vacation. Check out the drawers. There is a selection of emotions on either side.

Many of us do not connect what we do with how we go about it emotionally. We just do what we do in the way that we do it. (Even complaining or wishing for something else is part of how we go about life. We think we are changing something, yet little changes.) We find ourselves in the same type of relationship, or the same problems arise again, even when we change bosses, jobs, spouses, cities, countries, etc. We usually have a sense of our emotions, but do not see them as an influential force toward life's repeating patterns. The consequence? Without adding a different emotion to a situation, little will change in life over the long term.

The following awareness activities show us the connection between actions (what we tend to say and do) and emotions.

AWARENESS ACTIVITY
Your current emotional wardrobe

In this activity, we focus on your current emotional closet. What is there? What might be missing? You will take a broad look at your life through various frames, which are based on things that are common for people to care about.

Directions: Set aside 30 minutes and minimize distractions. There are three charts, each framed around familiar categories of responsibility: Career, Important Relationships, and Health/Well-being. On each chart, you will notice three columns.

Column 1: Review the areas of responsibility. Each is a domain in life that is important to take care of or pay attention to for overall well-being.

- Skip any areas that are not relevant or a part of your life now.
- In the blank spaces, add any area of responsibility that is not listed.

Column 2: Write the name of the emotion(s) that you associate with that area of responsibility.

- Make sure you select emotion(s) that represent what you feel *now*, NOT what you *want to feel*.
- NOTE: For ideas, you can use the list of emotions provided at the end of this section. These may or may not appropriately describe your emotions. Use words that fit your sensibilities.

Column 3: **As you think about the emotion(s) for each area, note any thoughts, judgments, etc.**

- Write what is so for you, and do not edit or "should" yourself.
- You are not committing to anything yet! Just observe and get used to seeing the influence of ever-present and missing emotions on your quality of life.

Career

Column 1	Column 2	Column 3
	Current Emotion(s)	Notes ... Thoughts ... Judgments ...
Work (Paid or unpaid)		
Profession (Or your life's mission)		
$ (Earning or using money)		
Add your own		

Important Relationships

Column 1	Column 2	Column 3
	Current Emotion(s)	Notes ... Thoughts ... Judgments ...
Spouse– Partner– Significant Other		
Children or Step-children		
Siblings		
Friends		
Add your own		

Health And Well-Being

Column 1	Column 2	Column 3
	Current Emotion(s)	Notes … Thoughts … Judgments …
Play/ Having fun		
Spirituality (Religion)		
Community/ Charity		
Fitness/ Exercise		
Add your own		

Personal Reflections

- Which emotion(s) are you wearing most often?
- Any missing or in short supply? (Any on the "emotions list" that you want a bit more of?)
- Do any "I used to…" or "I have not been lately" emotions come to mind?

_____

_____

_____

_____

_____

_____

_____

What suggestions do you have for yourself? (No commitments or decisions quite yet.) What are you taking away or what would you like to remember?

_____

_____

_____

_____

_____

_____

_____

_____

Emotions List

You can use this for ideas in filling out the charts. If this list does not quite hit the mark for you, but you aren't thinking of your own words either, consider using a dictionary or thesaurus to find words that are close to the following but more aptly articulate just what you want to say.

Ambitious	Goalless/Adrift	Raging/Enraged
Ambivalent	Guilty	Regretful
Angry	Hateful	Remorseful
Anxious	Hopeful	Respected
Ashamed	Hopeless	Respectful
Bored	Humiliated	Restless
Committed	Impatient	Sad
Compassionate	Indifferent	Satisfied
Complacent	Indignant	Self-pitying
Confused	Infatuated	Shy
Courageous/Bold	Interested	Skeptical
Covetous/Desirous	Jealous	Thankful
Curious	Joyful/Joyous	Wishful thinking
Despairing	Kindly	Wonder/Awe
Disappointed	Lonely	Add your own…
Dissatisfied	Nostalgic	
Dreading	Obsessive	
Embarrassed	Offended	
Enthusiastic	Patient	
Envious	Passionate	
Fearful	Peaceful	
Frustrated	Perplexed	
Generous	Prideful/Arrogant	

Author's Sample: April 2009

Work	Myopic/ Expectant	Lots on one plate with big project. No distractions!
Career/ Profession	Very satisfied!	Feel solid and competent and do what I love. I enjoy the groups I work with and the companies that provide them.
$	Curious	Since turning 60, am I winding down my earning years or extending them?
Play/ Having fun	Perplexity	Almost all my fun is in professional area and with spouse. I really enjoy both and don't feel like fun is missing. Is it? Hmmm. I like the question.
Spouse	Deeeeelight and Pride	Well married for 28 years. YUM!
Children	At peace	I am at peace with not having children.
Siblings	Okay … or Inattentive?	Again … sense of obligation coming from a "should" as well as a desire.
Friendships	Grateful (non-local) Wishful (local)	Have plenty of friends who live elsewhere and I would enjoy close local friends. Am I approaching resignation?
Health/ Well-being	Complacent or Disinterested?	Generally in good health. No energy to take on more here.
Community/ Charity	Content	I like the intermittent projects and working with the same nonprofit.
Spirituality (Religion)	Low level of anticipation	Feel a vague sense of a shift coming. Like a small seed not yet germinated.

Personal Reflections

I noticed my initial language was more dramatic than my actual experience. (I am a card-carrying member of the "not good enough" club and tend to be a bit dramatic. It seems a "not enough" life HAS to be yearning for something more and bigger.) That dramatic urgency influenced what I wrote initially. My "not good enough" took on a tone of ambivalence and expressed seemingly contradictory emotions. I am pleased that I took more time to "pin myself down" and write what was really so for me. I found I was more content than I tend to think. Now THERE'S a breath of fresh air!

Best *aha* moment? *I don't have to do it all right now. Whew.*

AWARENESS ACTIVITY
What in my emotional wardrobe have I been
wearing too much? Or too little?

With emotional agility, we have the opportunity to increase or decrease the intensity of our emotions. One way to speak about this intensity is with whom and how much we "wear an emotion." Go back and take a look at the illustration of the tortoise looking into its wardrobe (on page 27). Look at the differences between the right- and left-hand sides of the closet. What would life be like if you picked what to wear from the drawers on the left or the right for a day? Week? Month?

This section goes a bit further with that idea and helps you understand the nuances between varying degrees of resentment, resignation, acceptance, and ambition. Ultimately this understanding helps you decide what to do about situations in your life. For example: Will you stand for what you believe or let go for your own peace of mind? Cool down a bit when you are "too hot" to be effective or move to forgive? Increase the degree of intensity by speaking up vs. keeping your resentment to yourself = muteness? Forge ahead? Stand your ground? Scale back? Negotiate? Complain to a higher authority? Realize you expected something that was not promised? Withdraw your complaint? Make apologies for going too far? Etc.

In this activity, we continue to make connections between actions (what we do and do not do, say and do not say) and emotions. We'll take a close look at two familiar approaches to life: *opposition* and *acceptance.*

HAVE YOU BEEN WEARING RESENTMENT?

When we OPPOSE the PAST or PRESENT (what has and has not happened; what is or is not happening now), to varying degrees we enter resentment, disappointment, bitterness, or anger. When used to the right degree and for the right purpose, resentment fuels passions for justice or righting wrongs. However, for the never-enough crowd, resentment can take a darker or more unsatisfying turn. Without repeated points of satisfaction, we are easily irritated. When we persist with disliking, and cannot let go of what has or has not happened, we do not move forward. Even when we know or see what we are doing, we sometimes remain the same.

We live in the past, waiting for it and our future to change, and are perplexed as to why nothing changes. By revealing the patterns of a variety of emotions, we open the door to changing those patterns. For now, become an outside observer of some of the trends of the self-sacrificing, never-enough, overachiever crowd.

The language of resentment, dislike, annoyance, anger:

I don't like...   I hate...   I wish I/he/she/they had not...

That should not have happened.   This is wrong.   This is unfair.

I have been betrayed.   I have been fooled.

*Holding on to anger, resentment and hurt only gives you
tense muscles, a headache and a sore jaw from
clenching your teeth.* ~ Joan Lunden

✦

*Resentment is like taking poison and waiting for
the other person to die.* ~ Anonymous

✦

When anger comes, wisdom goes. ~ Hindi proverb

> **Carol's Coaching Corner:** My philosophy is that all emotions are valid—to some degree and in some situations. Take care not to judge an emotion as always good or always bad. (I thought resignation was an OK emotion while resentment was certainly NOT something a good person would ever want to express.) In the upcoming activities, you will actively look for where you have been over- or underdoing a set of emotions. At this point in the book, you are adding to your understanding of emotions and your current wardrobe.

How might we wear resentment out in the world?

We enter and prolong RESENTMENT with E-X-C-E-S-S:

- Accommodation. (Pleasers; saying yes when you mean no.)
- Duty. (Doing only from obligation, not feeling the rewards of being of service.)
- Anger, annoyance. (Staying on the negative side of life.)
- Bitterness, blaming. (Blaming as an attitude.)
- Blamelessness. (Tending to or trying to escape blame or responsibility. *It's not my fault.*)
- Controlling. (When others don't do things your way, anger or resentment arises.)
- Cynicism, disapproving, disgust, dislike, orneriness, or pessimism. (A pattern of being contrary vs. moving something forward.)
- Exhaustion, overwhelm. (From saying yes too often. *I'll do it.* Or saying yes when you mean no. *If I HAVE to.* Are you an offer machine? *Can I take that on? Let me.*)
- Expectations (Feel mostly entitled), impatience, testiness, vengefulness. (Think others owe you, as if they have made you a promise.)
- Frustration. (Without speaking up with requests or offers to move forward.)
- Muteness. (Not speaking up, suppressing your feelings, not asking for help.)

PERSONAL WORKSHEET

I enter and prolong RESENTMENT with TOO MUCH ...

_____

_____

_____

_____

_____

_____

_____

_____

_____

_____

Personal Reflections

_____

_____

_____

_____

_____

_____

_____

_____

_____

_____

INSIGHTS FROM OTHERS

When I did the resentment part, I remembered your story of discovering resentment. That hit me hard. Like you, I pretended everything was "fine" when it wasn't. My default was being mute. I did not speak up until I blew up like an overheated pressure cooker. I didn't want that kind of anger. I had no middle ground between rage and legitimate anger. Thank you for sharing the idea of speaking up much sooner about my disappointments.

My *aha* moment was about controlling. I prolong anger with my spouse, thinking she should somehow change to my liking. Lots of shoulds come out of my mouth. That in itself wasn't the best insight for me. I have known that about myself for some time. Visiting what my coercion feels like on her side, *that* was the insight. I don't give her a chance to say no. She has to say yes. I hate it when others do that to me.

HAVE YOU BEEN WEARING RESIGNATION?

When we are OPPOSED to POSSIBILITIES (what can or might happen), resignation, disappointment, and regret are triggered.

The language of resignation:

Why bother?   There is nothing you or anyone can do.

I can't because …   But …   There is no way out.   I have to …

They will never do that.   That might be okay for you, not for me.

In resignation, we resist, deny, or doubt the possibility of change.

How might we wear resignation out in the world?

We enter and prolong RESIGNATION with E-X-C-E-S-S:

- Anxiety, dread, fearfulness, fretting, gloom and doom, pessimism. (You speak or think often of what you are afraid of. Are you an "awful-izer" [someone who can, in a matter of minutes, predict many bad things happening]?)

- Boredom, disinterest. (You are waiting for something to happen to motivate you. Has the wait been too long?)
- Frustration, living as if you are bothered or burdened by life. (Poor me. Why me? Conforming—saying yes when you mean no.)
- Disappointment, dislike, skepticism, and stubbornness. (We are sure nothing is ever going to change, so why bother?)
- Distraction, drifting. (As in a pinball game, you bounce from one activity or "emergency" to another and are left feeling disillusioned, exhausted, or underappreciated.)
- Feeling obliged, quiet, tolerant. (Muteness; not speaking up.)
- Melancholy, regret, sadness, shame. (Viewing the past as better so the future looks grim.)

PERSONAL WORKSHEET
I enter and prolong RESIGNATION with TOO MUCH...

_____

_____

_____

_____

_____

_____

_____

_____

_____

Personal Reflections

_____

_____

_____

_____

_____

_____

_____

_____

INSIGHTS FROM OTHERS

Feeling obliged and forced to do what I HAD to do got my attention. I am wondering if I ever genuinely say yes. I live coerced by the wants, whining, and demands of others. I mostly remain quiet and put my head down and do it.

✦

Did you hear me swearing at you under my breath in class yesterday? I checked off seven boxes for resignation. Have you been living in my head? I was surprised at the amount of tolerating I am doing. As you suggested in class, I am doing LOTS of breathing.

HAVE YOU BEEN WEARING ACCEPTANCE?

Again the idea of the right balance of emotions helps us question if we have too little ambition or determination and too much accommodating or contentment. The focus shifts to understanding more about acceptance of the past. When we ACCEPT the PAST (what has and has not happened), contentment, acceptance, satisfaction, grace, and peace are available as emotions.

Acceptance does not mean condoning or liking. It has a sense of graciousness ... simply accepting that what is so is so. What has happened has happened.

The language of acceptance:

Even though that didn't happen, I am okay.   I forgive ...

I am at peace.   So be it.   I am letting go once and for all.

I accept the futility of hoping I/she/he/it/this will change.

*Forgiveness gives you back the laughter and the
lightness in your life.* ~ Joan Lunden

✦

One minute of patience, ten years of peace. ~ Greek proverb

✦

I have no regrets because I did my best—all I could do.
~ Midori Ito, Olympic skater

How might we wear acceptance out in the world?

We enter and prolong ACCEPTANCE with ENOUGH:

- Acceptance. (A sense of graciousness that maintains your dignity.)
- Serenity, a sense of stability.
- Accommodation, obliging. (Your dignity or sense of self is not compromised.)
- Admiration, appreciation. (Genuine and without pretense.)
- Contentment, peacefulness, quiet, tolerance. (From being at peace—not begrudging or jealous.)
- Caring for self and others, nurturing. (Not overdoing.)
- Being comfortable. (With yourself as you are and others as they are.)
- Conforming, cooperation. (Not excessive; just enough to feel at peace.)
- Feeling connected to and intentionally connecting to others or your own purpose.
- Open to delight, happiness, humor, joviality, playfulness, silliness.
- Nostalgia. (Fond memories.)
- Being okay with your sadness or regret. (With dignity.)
- Respect. (For self or others).
- Responsibility. (Managing commitments and not overdoing.)
- Trust. (Trusting others or being trustworthy.)

PERSONAL WORKSHEET

I enter and prolong ACCEPTANCE with ENOUGH...

_____

_____

_____

_____

_____

_____

_____

_____

_____

Personal Reflections

_____

_____

_____

_____

_____

_____

_____

_____

_____

_____

INSIGHTS FROM OTHERS

Thank you for the reminder that I do have the capacity for acceptance and calm. This exercise reminded me that I am okay, truly okay, with my divorce. I feel this huge opening for the future. Six months ago, I had no future, only acrimony. I was living within "should have and could have" with me, my ex, and what he stole from me and the kids. I am delighted to report that has lifted significantly.

Probably no shock to you, Carol, but my version of peace is active. I have avoided peace. For you it was fear of laziness; for me it was fear of boredom. Now, once a month, I have a purposeless Saturday. No plans. No to-do list. No nothing. I went out to the garden and actually enjoyed pulling weeds. I stopped before they were all gone because I wanted to. I took a nap in our hammock, which hadn't been used in years. Now there's a Saturday. Thanks.

HAVE YOU BEEN WEARING AMBITION?

For the self-sacrificing, never-enough, overachieving groups, ambition is both a helpful motivator and our enemy. There is a fine balance between going too far with our ambitions and having the right amount—aka What is enough ambition? This part of the activity supports you finding the right amount of ambition, at the right time and for the right purposes.

When we ACCEPT the FUTURE (what can and might happen), ambition, eagerness, and anticipation arise.

The language of ambition:

I can ...   Yes. I will ...   Sure!   May I ...?   What if I do ...?

If not _____, how about _____?

I promise to ...   I promise not to ...

I offer to ...   May I offer a suggestion?

If we will be quiet and ready enough, we shall find
compensation in every disappointment.
~ Henry David Thoreau

When the heart grieves over what it has lost,
the spirit rejoices over what it has left.
~ Sufi epigram

How might we wear the right amount of ambition out in the world?

We enter and prolong AMBITION with ENOUGH:

- Satisfaction (with accomplishments that energize), having accomplished (enough for today, on this project, for now).
- Admiration, awe.
- Calculating to, deciding to.
- Challenging, committing. (Enough yeses and enough noes.)
- Deciding to and deciding not to, determination (toward something or to an end goal).
- Confidence, respect (of self and others), trusting, trustworthiness, zestfulness.
- Being interested, connecting (to others or other tasks).
- Openness (to possibilities).
- Cooperating, conforming, being dutiful (in the way that brings joy or satisfaction; not fear, guilt, or anger).
- Courage, leading, (mentoring, parenting), pride, purpose, resolution, self-respect, striving.
- Creativity, curiosity, excitement, passion, expectancy (enthusiasm, not dread), exuberance, happiness, humor, joviality.
- Impatience, interest. (Ready to move on or forward.)
- Nurturing, tenderness.
- Optimism, passion, sense of responsibility that fills your heart and soul.

PERSONAL WORKSHEET
I enter and prolong AMBITION with ENOUGH...

Personal Reflections

INSIGHTS FROM OTHERS

My first challenge: What is enough? No kidding ... what IS enough? That is not a question I spend any time considering, much less answering. There's never enough time, resources, money to do this right, etc. (How's that for resentment!) Thank you for the satisfaction = enough action definition.

✦

Mine was enough striving. The worst offense? Always saying yes to our biggest customer. Our pride of delivering beyond expectations is killing us. Latest example? My head of technology noticed a pattern of their asking us for project changes on Thursday afternoon to be completed by the Monday morning caucus. (That means working over *every* weekend.) Our average work week is approaching 100 hours. Are we insane?

RECOGNIZING OUR EMOTIONAL PATTERNS

> *Men acquire a particular quality by constantly acting a particular way ... you become "just" by performing "just" actions, "temperate" by performing "temperate" actions, "brave" by performing "brave" actions.* - Aristotle

Once again, we take advantage of the notion that we are what we repeatedly do. What we do and how we go about doing it gives us clues to our emotional patterns. In this next activity, you will begin to recognize how much time you have been spending wearing the qualities and tendencies of very familiar emotional attitudes of our times— resentment, acceptance, resignation, and ambition. In the process, you will continue to see exactly how you acquire and wear these emotions day after day.

Carol's Coaching Corner: Our patterns are great revealers of why one's life is as it is. For some, these upcoming questions will bring surprises. (As I was surprised when I discovered I was a resentful person. My certainty regarding "how I thought I was" blinded me to the fact that I was behaving outside of my own beliefs.) For others, this may be a breath of fresh air. I offer this exercise in the spirit of revealing any blind spots you may have.

Can you create a safe space to see what you might not want to see about yourself? For example, send your version of an "itty bitty bitchy committee" away for the day. Leave your office. Turn off electronic devices. (I feel like a flight attendant.) Find a favorite reading spot or locale that tends to put you at ease. Begin recognizing that your environment influences how much (or little) you will learn. Multitasking is discouraged!

AWARENESS ACTIVITY

How much time are you spending in resentment, acceptance, resignation and ambition?

DIRECTIONS: Reflect on the question in each box. Put a percentage in each box that represents the amount of time you estimate having spent there *in the past week.*

You have 100% to distribute between the four boxes. Write specific examples of what you said, did, and did not do, next to the bullets (•). (SAMPLE provided at end.)

Opposing the past and/or present ➔ RESENTMENT

How much of your time do you spend opposing or disliking the past and/or present?

Resentful toward – Angry at – Disappointed in

_____%

My examples:

-
-
-
-
-

Accepting the past and/or present ➔ PEACE

How much of your time do you spend accepting the past and or present?

Accepting of – Grateful for – Okay with – Satisfied with – Gracious about

_____%

My examples:

-
-
-
-
-

Personal Reflections

Reflect on how you interacted with the past and/or present:

Surprises? "Oh my!" moments?

_____

_____

_____

_____

_____

What about your patterns do you like?

_____

_____

_____

_____

_____

What about your patterns do you dislike?

_____

_____

_____

_____

_____

Opposing the future → RESIGNATION

**How much of your time do you spend
opposing or disliking the future?**

*Resigned about – Disappointed with –
Desires that cannot be fulfilled*

_____%

My examples:

-
-
-
-
-

Accepting the future → AMBITION

**How much of your time do you spend embracing
or being eager for the future?**

Ambition for – Desire to – Eager to

_____%

My examples:

-
-
-
-
-

Personal Reflections

Reflect on how you interacted with the future:

Surprises? "Oh my!" moments?

_____

_____

_____

_____

_____

_____

What about your patterns do you like?

_____

_____

_____

_____

_____

What about your patterns do you dislike?

_____

_____

_____

_____

_____

Carol's Coaching Corner: Take heart if you find yourself a bit disappointed, frustrated, regretful, or in any number of other emotions that take us off balance. By knowing more specifically *what* is out of balance and *how* you stay there, you will be able to choose to stay there *or*, when ready, take different actions and move on to something more appealing.

Having choices is empowering. Without this kind of active awareness, your choices are limited to what you know now. Consider being patient and kind to yourself when your critical self arises.

Let this activity serve your *best intentions for yourself.*

Author's Sample:

Opposing the past and/or present ➜ RESENTMENT
60%
• Again this week, I said yes to my boss for staying late and no to plans I'd made for finally going home on time. • That put me over 60 hrs again. As an executive, I am exempt from overtime. I resent that I am expected to work 60+ hours a week "to be a team player." • Yesterday, my boss said she loved what I designed. Then I heard her say "but this could be better" three times. Nothing is ever enough here. • The GM came in today and said he wanted me to do something next week. I said I was on vacation. He said, no problem, I could do it via email. I resent that they even expect me to work on vacations. I am angry at myself for not saying ANYTHING.

Accepting of the past and/or present ➜ PEACE
15%
• I heard recently that others take weekends off. I was so sure no one else did, I didn't ask. I now see weekend work as a choice. • Although my GM expects me to watch out for his project while on vacation, that does NOT mean I have to do other work.

Opposing the future ➜ RESIGNATION

20%

- I cannot change how it is and likely will be around here.
- Why waste my time caring? Why should I work harder than others?

Accepting the future ➜ AMBITION

5%

Someday I will slow down. (Truthfully, I am halfhearted on this point.)

Personal Reflections:

Biggest aha moments? 1) I don't speak up. When angry, I go mute and then explode on the drive home, or worse yet, at home. 2) I can speak up after I cool down instead of in the heat of the moment. On vacation, I had a very doable amount of work (which I did after dinner) and didn't interrupt sitting by the pool!

PERSONAL WORKSHEET
Your patterns and tendencies

Overall, insofar as resentment, acceptance, resignation, and ambition, what did you learn about your patterns and tendencies?

_____

_____

_____

_____

_____

_____

_____

Optional Activity: Make some changes for the next week

If you were to decrease and increase between the categories by a total of 5–10% next week, what would you do differently? (Start doing? Stop doing?)

- Be specific. Put something on your calendar.
- Keep the percentages adding up to 100%.

_____

_____

_____

_____

_____

_____

Where to from here?

In Step 2 our emotional agility extends to the emotions often missing for those saving our inner tortoise: peace of mind, joy,   wholeheartedness, contentment or being genuinely satisfied.

Ready for some R and R (rest and relaxation)? Turn the page.

STEP 2: GIVE YOUR SELF-SACRIFICING, NEVER-ENOUGH, OVERACHIEVING TORTOISE A BREAK

In Step 1 I introduced the concept of life and emotions as patterns. Getting more of the same in life is a direct and predictable consequence of what we repeatedly say and do and the emotions influencing us along the way. Through the lenses of resentment, resignation, ambition, and acceptance, you saw not only the emotions you have been wearing, but also the actions you tend to take when wearing those emotions.

In Step 2 you will actively change what you repeatedly do. This step is for those who want to see change *now*. No more of the same. To some extent you are willing to remove your own version of the helmet and rocket strapped to your back. You will be rewarded with an increased ability to notice and change your patterns. Along the way, new emotions will arrive. Ultimately you will be able to make more choices about your daily life experience by choosing which patterns and emotions to extend and which to leave behind for a while.

Carol's Coaching Corner: If we stubbornly or blindly continue to do and say what we have been doing and saying, how can we expect a different future? Expecting others to change because they should, or because it is their fault your life is as it is, could be a long wait.

If you prefer quicker results, try the upcoming activities.

ACTIVATING AN EMOTION

At this stage, emotional agility consists of increasing your trust and curiosity so that you can indeed shift from one emotional state to another. How? Introducing activating an emotion. Authors Paul Ekman and Richard Davidson offer:

> In the course of our research, we found something that surprised us. If you intentionally make a facial expression, you change your physiology. By making the correct expression, you begin to have the changes in your physiology that accompany the emotion. The face is not simply a means of display, but also a means of activating emotion.

This is strictly voluntary—but these expressions turn on the involuntary system. In other words, simply putting the face into a smile drives the brain to activity typical of happiness—just as a frown does with sadness. [6]

Following are some short, simple, and voluntary activities that are *guaranteed* to activate an emotion.

Carol's Coaching Corner: I cannot force you to learn. My task in this section is to get you started and give you hints for success. Your task is to give these activities a good try.

For many of you, once or twice will suffice to increase a sense of well-being and increase your trust in emotional agility. Others, like me initially, who are good at doubting and at not following instructions, may have to make several attempts to succeed.

How long the shift lasts and how often the sense of well-being returns is up to you. Your sincerity and curiosity go a long way to initiate shifts that prove meaningful. I have provided a number of insights from others to give you ideas of what is possible.

Success Factors

Here is some wisdom collected from clients, students, and my own experimenting:

- **Perfection is NOT required.** Do the activities with the best effort you can muster. Some fumbling or self-consciousness in the beginning is to be expected. Can you enjoy being a beginner at something again?
- **Trust the process.** For a few minutes, suspend having to know beforehand what will happen or why it happens. This is especially needed when you have been disappointed in yourself or life to a fair degree. Overthinking and analyzing s-l-o-w-s the benefits.
- **Do not discount the simplicity.** When immersed in the doldrums, that part of your self is *the worst person* to advise you

what will work. Let your inner wisdom of wanting a greater sense of well-being have its voice. As one student offered: "I can't believe it's so simple. And I'll take it." Let the simplicity work for you.

- **Set aside *shoulds, should haves* and *could haves,* and *unfulfilled wishes.*** Don't worry. If you miss them, you can bring them back.

SIMPLE PRACTICE #1
Breathe

- Stop what you are doing and become aware of your breathing.
- Take three long and even breaths.
- Equal breaths in and out.
- Counting helps to maintain a rhythm. Equal counts for the inhale and exhale.
- What did you notice? What automatically happened with your posture? Face? Eyes? Cheeks? Jaw?
- Repeat three more long and even breaths. Again, what did you notice?
- Go back to what you were doing.

INSIGHTS FROM OTHERS

My yoga teacher told me it is impossible to sustain stress or anxiety while breathing fully, slowly, and deeply. She was right!

✦

My biggest *aha*—gift really—was to recognize I was very new to actively relieving my own doldrums. I found myself in familiar anger that seemed impossible to get out of ... I did stick with the breathing pattern, and after four tries felt the tension release from my shoulders and jaw and my anger gone.

All I can say now is: patience ... the relief WILL come! Just follow the instructions.

SIMPLE PRACTICE #2
Smile

1. **Smile. Yes, right now ... smile. Before second-guessing. Just try it.**

   - Feel the outside edges of your mouth *and* eyes pulling upward. Feel your eyes widen.
   - Let the mouth and eyes smile. Keep them there.
   - Raise your chin so that your eyes naturally look up and out.
   - Breathe in even, rhythmic breaths.
   - Let the rest of your body feel the smile! (Release any tension in shoulders, arms, neck. Sit back or stand up, wiggle or move around to release other tensions.)

Carol's Coaching Corner: Nothing to smile about? See if you can, as Dr. Ekman suggested, voluntarily activate your brain toward happiness by smiling. The brain doesn't need a logical reason to activate an emotion. The body (in this case your face) supports you in activating.

---

2. **Can you hold a sincere smile for two minutes?**

   - Let the feeling of a good smile wash over you. Notice what happens physically and emotionally while you're wearing a sincere smile.
   - When you realize you are no longer smiling, simply bring the smile back—raise the outer edges of your eyes and mouth. Let the smile happen. No drama. No disappointments. Simply return to smiling. Let yourself feel genuine smile energy.

SMILE OPTIONS

- **Like what happened? Want more?** Do these smile practices 3–5 times a day *in private* until you can do them with relative ease and a good dose of sincerity. Then do them while around other people. Smile at anyone who smiles at you. Smile and see if you can get others to smile back. (Sincerity is key. Smile and mean it.)
- **How long can you maintain a sincere smile?** What's next in your day? Try to keep a smile on your face for the next 5–10 minutes. Try smiling while doing life's daily and mundane tasks:
- **Smile while dressing for the day,** taking a shower, or getting ready for bed.
- **Grin while preparing a meal,** cleaning up afterwards, or traveling to work.

The more mundane the activity the better. The fact that you know how to do something automatically allows you to pay attention to bringing a smile to the effort. It is *how* you are going about it, not *what* you are doing.

- When you realize you are no longer smiling, smile. Let yourself feel smile energy.

Carol's Coaching Corner: Feel silly, out of sorts, uncomfortable? Not that surprising if much of life is difficult or disappointing. That you are feeling silly or out of sorts is actually a good sign. (You are intentionally bringing forth something new. You are shifting out of your norm.) *Congratulations!*

SIMPLE PRACTICE #3

Eyebrows Up!

Turn on one of your involuntary systems and give yourself an emotional lift by simply raising your eyebrows!

- Open your eyelids. A bit wider! What's the right amount of openness to feel a lift?
- Give yourself a face-lift! Remove any wrinkles between your eyebrows. Add a sparkle in your eye and a small smile for good measure.
- Can you stay angry, sad, or disappointed with raised eyebrows and a sparkle in your eye?

Carol's Coaching Corner: This may be a temporary lift! Sometimes we really are beginners at well-being or are prone to anger or sadness. Play with the idea of taking some of the intensity out of life. You may not call it intensity … it is your reality. But give lightness, an increased sense of well-being, and happiness a good try.

SIMPLE PRACTICE #4

Grumpiness or happiness—your choice!

This practice introduces the idea of "entering" and "exiting" an emotion. You will activate several emotions by doing an opposites activity with faces!

Take a few slow deep breaths and be ready to notice an emotion.

STEP 1: Mimic the face below.

1. Look in a mirror and use your facial muscles, forehead, eyebrows, cheeks, and jaw to "copy" the face above.

2. What emotion(s) "come" with this face?

3. Allow yourself to enter your version of the emotion. To maintain it, what must you do with the outside edges of your eyes? Forehead? Jaw? Cheeks?

4. Next, exaggerate! Use the rest of your body to accentuate the emotion. (Posture, shoulders, breathing pattern.) Allow your whole body to align with the emotions!

5. Stay there for two minutes.

Notice what happens for you:
- What thoughts and feelings arise?
- Any memories from the past?
- What about the future? If you were to spend the rest of the day or week in this face, body, and emotion, what would life be like?

STEP 2: STOP! Activate a "neutral" emotion.

Interrupt whatever emotions or thoughts arise by taking a few slow deep breaths. Adjust your posture and sit or stand erect. Move your body around or wiggle from head to toe. Take any frown off your face and furrow from your forehead to activate a more neutral facial expression. No frown/no smile.

STEP 3: Mimic the face below.

1. Look in a mirror and use your facial muscles, forehead, eyebrows, cheeks, and jaw to "copy" the face above.

2. What emotion(s) "come" with this face?

3. Allow yourself to enter your version of the emotion. To maintain it, what must you do with the outside edges of your eyes? Forehead? Jaw? Cheeks?

4. Next, exaggerate! Use the rest of your body to accentuate the emotion (posture, shoulders, breathing pattern). Allow your whole body to align with the emotion.

5. Stay there for two minutes.

Notice what happens for you:
- Is this a familiar face and feeling for you?
- What thoughts arise? Any memories from the past?
- What about the future? If you were to spend the rest of the day or week in this face, body, and emotion, what would life be like?

STEP 4: Repeat

Repeat Steps 1-3 until you can enter and exit the emotions by adjusting your face and body.

Which emotion do you choose for the rest of today?

What would you have to do with your face and the rest of your body and attitude to keep the selected emotion going for the rest of today?

INSIGHTS FROM OTHERS

To be honest, I didn't like how easy it was to change my emotional state. Seems I have to take more responsibility for my life experiences. I'll have to think about this more.

✦

I didn't want to try this smile thing with people I knew. It felt somehow insincere or fake. (I discovered after doing this for a while that my smiling had, for some time, been a pretense.) Although embarrassed at the truth of my motives, I really did want to be less of a fake, so I focused on smiling with gratitude. Carol reminded me to keep it simple. It was easy to smile and mean it when I said thank you to the gas station cashier, the cheery toll operators, and the dry cleaning man. Looking them in the eye was important. That they were brief encounters helped as well. (I really did need to practice being grateful.)

What I didn't expect was that people started smiling at me first. Had they always been smiling and I ignored them??? Graciousness appeared as if by magic. (People holding doors open for me or letting me have the parking space. Was this connected? Had I really been that grumpy or unapproachable? Not sure and I don't really care—I like the feeling of grace.)

✦

While doing the neutral or in-between emotion, I noticed my shoulders tended to be up near my ears. I had to lower them to be more at ease. I stopped wearing my shoulders as earrings! (Who knew how tense I was???!) A feeling of tenderness appeared and tears welled up. Not sad tears ... Do sweet and grateful tears make sense?

✦

I tried eyebrows up, and found curiosity bubbled up! I immediately got a flash of the face of my four-year-old nephew when he was at my house this summer. When around my cats and my dog, his face expressed a bit of wonder, apprehension, curiosity, and play all rolled into one. His "predisposition"? MOVE forward, taking it all in, and not taking falls or missteps too seriously. I saw the face of wide-eyed wonder and whole person learning. I played with mimicking his face and attitude and found a joy I hadn't felt in a while. He's a pretty good joy coach!

✦

I tried a smiling practice earlier this week ... and found that it starts to actually "stick" after a while. Today I found myself spontaneously smiling in the midst of waiting in line at the grocery store with a bunch of grumpy shoppers. I actually enjoyed myself!

✦

I liked the eyebrows up one. It is a lot cheaper (and less risky) than Botox!

INTERRUPT OLD PATTERNS WITH NEW PATTERNS

One swallow does not make a summer, neither does one fine day; similarly one day or brief time of happiness does not make a person entirely happy. ~ Aristotle

I suspect you have a better idea of what Aristotle is offering here now that you've practiced with emotional agility by activating the emotions I chose in the earlier exercise. This next section gives you more options of how to make your own choices. You will be taking repeated vacations from your previous patterns.

Key elements of emotional agility are: 1) noticing our habits and patterns, and 2) interrupting those patterns with different patterns.

Carol's Coaching Corner: The more at ease you are with these interruptions, the faster and easier implementing change becomes. In these early steps, my intent is to make emotional agility fast, easy, and enjoyable to learn. Long-term change in your life is unlikely at this point.

In this part, fast and easy *are* the success factors. Sustainability will come later.

SIMPLE PRACTICE
Opposites activities

This idea is a simple one: Do the opposite of something you normally do.

Rule #1: Whatever practice you choose, do it for 7 days or 7 times in a row. If you miss one day or occurrence, the count starts over!

Rule #2: Do the "Opposite Simple Practice" you choose long enough to feel it as a new pattern. I suggest 7 days. If that is not long enough, extend the time.

Rule #3: Keep a log of your awareness and insights.

Make your bed every day?

Leave it unmade for 7 days in a row.

OR

Never make your bed?

Make it every day for 7 days in a row.

Other options of patterns to interrupt: dishes, housecleaning, exercise, homework, practicing an instrument, cooking vs. eating out.

Wear a watch?

Wear your watch on the opposite wrist for 7 days.

OR

Do not wear your watch for 7 days.

Abstinence

(**Note:** This is NOT to deprive yourself. Abstain from something to *enliven* another aspect of your life! Feel free to give up something that makes it possible to add what you want more of in life.)

Think of something you "cannot do without."

Abstain and do without it for 7 days in a row.

Examples: TV – video games – computer – email – texting – chocolate – a beverage or food habit – reading

Brush your teeth?

Brush your teeth with the opposite hand for 7 days in a row.

Take the same route to work or school?

For 7 days in a row, take a different route or form of transportation than you normally do. Mix it up even more by doing one thing one day and something else the next day.

Feel overwhelmed?

Say yes when you mean no? Feel coerced or forced in life?

*Like a daily vitamin, say "No" or "No thank you" calmly
and with dignity once a day for 7 days in a row.*

Exhausted?

*For 7 days in a row, stop and take slow, deep breaths for 3 minutes during
every waking hour. (Set an alarm if needed.)*

Have your own ideas? Go for it!

PERSONAL WORKSHEET
Interrupting your patterns

Make a daily log of your awareness and insights. What was it like to interrupt yourself? What emotions arose before, during, and after interrupting a habit?

Day 1

_____

_____

_____

Day 2

_____

_____

_____

Day 3

_____

_____

_____

Day 4

_____

_____

_____

Day 5

_____

_____

_____

_____

Day 6

_____

_____

_____

_____

Day 7

_____

_____

_____

_____

Personal reflections

While a profound _aha_ moment is not required from these activities, what _did_ you see and learn about yourself and your patterns?

- **Are there any patterns you adopted some time ago that are outdated or no longer useful?**

_____

_____

_____

_____

- Are any of your habits "chosen" for you by outside influences? (Parents, colleagues, bosses, professions, organizations, economic circumstances, age, gender, marital status, etc.?)

_____

_____

_____

_____

- What patterns are you considering changing for good or for an extended period?

_____

_____

_____

_____

- Any patterns you wish to extend or use in different circumstances or in your interactions with other people?

_____

_____

_____

_____

INSIGHTS FROM OTHERS

Carol, I thought you were crazy suggesting I stop wearing a watch. (I have important meetings to get to and train schedules to meet.) I learned three things about myself with this exercise: First, I tend to compete with time. I jam as much as I can into every single minute. (If I am early to a meeting, I pull out my Blackberry and squeeze in a few emails. I am often late to that same meeting because I got distracted.)

Second, God forbid I'd stop to enjoy something from arriving early. No wonder I feel pushed in life. I am the pusher!

Finally, it is easy to find out what time it is! Clocks and people with watches are everywhere. Predominant emotions? I traveled through anxiety (Could I trust others to be on time?), regret (I wished I would have learned this earlier in life), and eventually felt more at ease. (I no longer wear a watch. I like the feeling of freedom.)

✦

Surely my mother was rolling over in her grave when I stopped making my bed! This was the first of several "rules" I discovered I live by without choosing for myself. After the week, I found I actually liked a made bed instead of feeling it as a *have to*. Emotionally I traveled from feeling obligated to feeling freer as I make my bed. FASCINATING ... same bed—VERY different quality of life. I am curious about what else I feel obligated by that I could actually enjoy.

✦

You mentioned in class that you were a recovering "yes machine." That hit home for me. Considering saying "no" was a profound shift for me. It revealed how much I do out of fear. Fear of displeasing, disapproval, being disliked, or worse yet, being fired. I had a fear habit!!! Just the idea of saying "no" sent shivers down my spine. (My boss acts as if someone will die if I don't do what he asks NOW!)

I admit I could not muster the courage to "just say no." So, I invented my own exercise—"Not Until." (I can't do that until next Thursday. If you need it earlier, then _____ will wait until _____. What is the priority?) I used this "not until" with my boss, I wasn't fired, and nobody died.

I liked this so much that I started doing it with my team when they seemed overwhelmed. Funny, I now trust their yeses. They seemed to learn "no" *much* faster than I could. At first, it was disconcerting. What if they never said yes when I really needed them to? That tends not to be the case. Less overwhelm seems to cultivate willingness to do extra when asked. My assistant was one of the first to use "not until" on me. Yesterday, she OFFERED to do something for me. (A first for her. Before

I always piled on the work and she always said yes and worked long hours.) She actually goes home on time now with a smile. I am grateful for leaving my fear habit for only fleeting moments of anxiety. What's next for me? This exercise pointed out how many "relationships" I am tolerating to please someone else. Saying "no" seems more practical now, even appealing, than it did two weeks ago when I started this. The fear habit is dissolving before my eyes.

✦

I went on a TV fast. I was inspired by a Buddhist monk I met on a peace walk. He was on a 20-day food fast—to clear his mind. While I won't give up food, I decided I would fast from TV. I didn't watch anything for an entire week, and guess what?—WAY more energy. I've been practicing flute and piano, reading, catching up with friends, cooking—usually I would have picked one of these and then decided to squish it in between commercial breaks. I feel so much more satisfied with each day and have spent time and attention on things I have been saying I want to devote time to, but never seemed to get around to. I allowed myself one break from the "fast" and am going to continue and see what happens. Being on the road will be an interesting test, since one of the first things I usually do when I get to a hotel is flip on the tube.

MOODS VS. EMOTIONS: A SUBTLE YET IMPORTANT DIFFERENCE

We "visit" emotions for a time. They are temporary and tend to "arrive" when something happens. An event triggers the emotion. In the midst of a busy day we find ourselves happy with a text or phone call from a friend, upset after a complaint from a customer or colleague, delighted by an unexpected financial windfall, or anxious about an upcoming event. What happens with you and others in the car with a flat tire? What happens when you are late? What about the people who are waiting for you? How about when your printer jams? When it starts working again?

Each of these events activates some emotion. If you notice, you will find that the change in emotion typically lasts as long as the event. When you get back to your routine, that other emotion disappears. Once the event and emotion are over, you return to homeostasis—your "home" mood. (Once the flat tire is fixed and you are on your way, or when the printer jam is over, you are back in business.)

Moods are emotions that last longer. Moods hang around and come back without our asking or choosing. Why? We've spent weeks, months, years, and maybe decades practicing them. Their frequency increases our susceptibility to their being activated. Remember the patterns and tendencies of optimism and pessimism? Remember the activities in Step 1 with resentment, resignation, ambition, and peace? Our moods and everyone else's moods are predispositions for action. We often do not notice our own mood or even name it as a mood. Instead, we see pessimism or optimism, resentment or peace, sadness or happiness, anger or calm as our *reality*. If we live in them month after month or year after year, that is a mood.

"Pervasive" is a good word for moods: they affect how we see, what we say and don't say. (We're like a fish that doesn't know it is swimming in polluted water.) Our moods are mostly transparent. We ARE them.

The trick is to realize that our "reality" is influenced by the mood and emotions we embody over time. What "seems" so true just might change if we adjust our emotion or mood. You will experience this difference as you do some of the activities throughout this book.

When in an emotion, we are predictable. Emotions predispose us to take certain actions and not others. ***In a way, our emotions choose for us.*** In a culture where many of us like to feel special, unique, and think we should have a choice in all that we do, this idea of predictability may generate some resistance. Like it or not, when in an emotion we follow recognizable patterns, and those patterns influence the choices we can and cannot make.

Carol's Coaching Corner: Other ways of talking about emotional predictability are as mindsets or personality traits. I emphasize using these new terms so we do not fall back into the assumptions from our old language patterns, thus paving the way to easier learning. The important point at this juncture is how we follow certain patterns when in an emotion.

Think you are not very predictable? Our siblings, children, parents, friends, and colleagues are aware of our emotional patterns— sometimes more than we are! Are you curious enough to ask them? How might they describe your emotional patterns?

- You are such a happy-go-lucky person or you seem down.
- We can always count on you for your _____ (humor, insightfulness, caring manner, strength, bringing us back down to earth, inspiration).
- You are often _____ (skeptical, critical, doubting, resistant, deflecting responsibility, etc.).

Would their characterizations match yours?

Look at the charts on the next two pages to see the patterns of predictability of two familiar emotions—optimism and pessimism:

	Optimism
Definition	Disposed to take a favorable view of events or conditions and to expect the most favorable outcome.
Emotional "cousins"	Buoyant, Certain, Happy, Encouraging, Hopeful, Trusting.
Behaviors of optimists...	Most often cheerful. Easygoing. Confident, hopeful. Positive, a sunny disposition. Do not stay "down" or discouraged too long. Tend not to worry, or if they do worry, they take action. Often overlook or ignore negatives. Expect the best.
Optimists often say...	Yes. And. Can. I/We could... Might. Sure. Let's try anyway. Let's look at the positives. What else could we do? I'll try (and mean it). That's challenging *and*... I want hope instead of being so realistic.
Optimists say *less* often...	No. But. Can't. Shouldn't. I doubt it. Why bother? That is a bad (or dumb) idea. That won't work either. I did and it didn't work. I'll try but...
Optimists often...	Make offers or volunteer. Jump on board. Request help. Come up with ideas, more ideas, and even more ideas.
Optimists rarely...	Wait to be asked, told, or ordered to do something. As such, they may not want to stop creating ideas. It can be hard to know when enough is enough.
Physical tendencies...	Ready smile. Wrinkle in forehead (curiosity for problem solving). Sparkle in eye. Open posture. Forward motion. Action oriented. Moving.

	Pessimism
Definition	A tendency to stress the negative, unfavorable, or to take the gloomiest possible view.
Emotional "cousins"	Healthy skepticism, Hopeless, Doubtful, Dejected, Disappointed
Behaviors of pessimists...	Tend to worry. Can look gloomy, bored, or hopeless. Can be ironic, derisive, doubtful, disbelieving. Can be looked to for critical thinking. Expect the worst.
Pessimists often say...	No. But. Can't. Shouldn't. I doubt it. Let's be realistic. Okay (without meaning it). Why bother? That's a bad (or dumb) idea. That won't work either. I tried and it didn't work. I'll try *but...* (with a tone of *won't work*.)
Pessimists tend *not* to say...	Yes (and mean it). And. Can. Could. Might. Sure. Let's try anyway. Let's look at the positives. What else could we do? I'll try (and mean it). That's challenging and...
Pessimists often...	Wait to be asked or told. Offer few ideas. Shoot down ideas. Help to know when to stop.
Pessimists rarely...	Do something because it is new or novel. Offer or volunteer. Jump on board quickly. Request help. (A part of resignation's "Why bother?") Come up with ideas.
Physical tendencies...	Wrinkle in forehead (worry). Tight shoulders or stance. Contained or contracted energy. Can sit back with scowl in silence or actively oppose.

EMOTIONAL REVERBERATION:
WE HAVE THE CHOICES OUR EMOTION ALLOWS!

As we saw with optimism and pessimism, when in an emotion, the pattern is obvious—well, obvious to some! We all can recognize optimistic, pessimistic, bad-tempered, cheery, mean, or delightful when we see it. We can even see it coming down the hall or listen to it over the phone or in an email/text.

If this is true for the way we see others, it is true for the way they see us as well. However, we are often blind to our own emotions. Remember my story of discovering I was a resentful person? (In the "Good to Know…" section.) My own resentment only became clear to me when I stopped to reflect on my patterns of blame. Prior to that, as a "good girl" I accepted my resignation as true, never realizing that resentment and not speaking up was eroding a good work relationship over time.

The same is likely true for some of your emotional patterns. Like me, you tend *not* to call it an emotion. You simply live it, or say that is how life is for you—and will likely always be. In *A General Theory of Love,* the authors speak of *emotional reverberation*—where a dominant emotion influences what is seen and not seen; done and not done; said and not said:

> Gleeful people automatically remember happy times, while a depressed person effortlessly recalls incidents of loss, desertion, and despair. Anxious people dwell on past threats; paranoia instills a retrospective preoccupation with situations of persecution.
>
> If an emotion is sufficiently powerful, it can quash opposing networks so completely that their content becomes inaccessible—blotting our discordance section of the past. Within the confines of that person's virtuality, those events didn't happen. [7]

Emotions are a filter through which we see, do, and feel. This filter influences how we speak about the past, present, and future. It affects the decisions we make. (Who we date and marry. The jobs we apply for. The customers we seek.) Until the emotion changes, the filters stay as they are. That works just fine until your emotional wardrobe falls short on variety.

For example, when you are completing a task or project, ambition is a handy emotion to put on. It allows us to focus on a goal, remove distractions, and finish something on time and/or within budget. Within fully operating ambition, any mistakes from the past go into the background. The future is defined by goals and we focus on taking action.

Ambition's reverberation is clear: There is an end in sight and we work toward it. We do whatever it takes. We sacrifice whatever is needed. In terms of our emotional wardrobe, after completion, we can put the ambition back in the closet for use later. Its time or usefulness has passed. It will be ready for us when we need it again.

What happens if we do not take ambition off? What if we wear it at home, with friends, on vacation? Some of us know exactly what happens. We overdo doing! We say yes, yes, yes. We say yes even when people have not asked us specifically to do anything. We bring our work home every night, on weekends, and with us on vacation. We have very good reasons for doing this. *This is too important … I'll stop soon. I am exhausted but…*

The benefits of ambition begin to disappear the more we wear it. We do not even call it ambition—it's just how we "do" life. Whether necessary or not, our head is down, our eyes are narrowly focused, and we forge ahead. We do not see that our relationships suffer because of our "ambitious habit." We do not see that we are missing life around us. Sometimes we *do* see what our overachieving ways are doing to us; however, it is a brief glance, and we return to our normal ambitious ways.

Is there something wrong with us if we cannot change our emotions at will? Is it a character flaw perhaps? Thankfully, no. We are simply experiencing the aforementioned *emotional reverberation.*

RECOGNIZING THE PATTERNS OF OPTIMISM AND PESSIMISM

As emotional beings, we have an innate wisdom and common sense about our emotional lives. We are smarter than we might think about the patterns of emotions. As was mentioned before, we KNOW when we or someone else is happy, irritated, angry, or playful. However, in terms of shifting emotions, what tends to happen first is that our emotions "have us"—Emotional reverberation. We find ourselves in an emotion after it has already begun. Without practicing emotional agility, shifting emotions becomes more of a challenge.

The goal of these upcoming activities is to show how much we already know about emotions and how they predispose us to think, feel, and do as a result. This way of observing will become indispensable when designing ways of being more emotionally agile by:

- Recognizing tendencies, behaviors, and characteristics of different emotions. (Optimism is not necessarily better than pessimism. Both have advantages and both have consequences.)
- Getting to know how we cultivate emotions (and make them last longer).
- Giving us hints about what we can do to leave them behind

Here are some quotes that reveal how much we already know about optimism and pessimism.

Both optimists and pessimists contribute to our society.
The optimist invents the airplane and the pessimist the parachute.
~ Gladys Bronwyn Stern

✦

A pessimist sees the difficulty in every opportunity;
an optimist sees the opportunity in every difficulty.
~ Sir Winston Churchill

✦

The optimist proclaims that we live in the best of all possible
worlds; and the pessimist fears this is true.
~ James Branch Cabell

✦

Optimists view life as a glass half full.
Pessimists view life as a glass half empty.
~ Anonymous

AWARENESS ACTIVITY
Optimism and pessimism in others

Think of one person you know whom you would describe as optimistic. Think of a second person whom you would describe as pessimistic. These can be colleagues, friends, bosses, even family members. Write your response to each question in the space provided. (Refer back to the pessimism and optimism charts for hints.)

How does each person approach changes, new ideas, problems, and surprises?

The Optimist	The Pessimist

What do you expect them to do or say? (For example, in a meeting, on vacation, at the start or end of a project?)

The Optimist	The Pessimist

What behavior or remark would surprise you?

The Optimist	The Pessimist

How do *you* feel when around them?

The Optimist	The Pessimist

Emotional reverberation in action! We all have our emotional filters. You have just indicated what *you* see as the resulting behaviors from pessimism and optimism.

Carol's Coaching Corner: Does your seeing them in this way mean it is true? Not necessarily. Emotional reverberation was also in play in *you* when you answered these questions. Your own emotion shapes how you answered.

Your own emotional filters affect how you see others and how you automatically react when you are around them. Remember the quote about gleeful people automatically remembering happy times?

No matter our emotional "home base," we tend to feel right or justified there—after all, that IS how the world IS.

Maybe not…

How might you take advantage of a change in perception? In our optimism or pessimism, instead of saying "that IS how the world IS" consider that is how I tend to see the world through that emotion. That it is your current predisposition, given your current emotional wardrobe. A different emotional setting for you could literally change how you see a situation, friend, or colleague. For example, before seeing how resentful I was, I was in the throes of resentment, wondering why my relationships were difficult. It never occurred to me that I was contributing to the difficulties by blaming everyone else for my unhappiness. Emotional awareness opens the door to change.

PERSONAL WORKSHEET
Optimism and pessimism in yourself

Respond to any or all of the following questions to expand your understanding of your emotional patterns.

- Would you characterize yourself as predisposed to optimism or pessimism?
- What might be the advantages of optimism? Disadvantages?
- What might be the advantages of pessimism? Disadvantages?
- What reaction might an optimistic person have to pessimistic ones? (For example, an optimistic team member meeting with a pessimistic one?)
- What reaction might a pessimistic person have to an optimistic one?

_____

_____

_____

_____

_____

_____

_____

_____

_____

_____

_____

_____

TRYING ON OPTIMISM AND PESSIMISM

Consider before you begin... ALL emotions are valid, legitimate, and useful in *some* (and not all) circumstances. They all serve some purpose—and that includes even those we deem negative. For example, sadness about a loss points us to how we cared. Boredom shows us a lack of action or points toward passion missing in us. If your team is full of optimists or pays little attention to any pessimists, you may miss the pessimists' critical eye for what might not work. You will likely find out too late if their skepticism was well founded. The opposite is true with a team of pessimists. As we saw with the charts, skepticism and a habit of "no" slows or stops progress.

Ultimately, we are seeking to update your emotional wardrobe. In order to do that, you must try on new and varied emotions!

Carol's Coaching Corner: If you tend to be optimistic, you might feel a bit of resistance or be perplexed in this activity. Your optimistic self may wonder, *What good is pessimism? Those people are such "downers."* Try pessimism and see its advantages. Some situations need a more critical eye.

If, on the other hand, you tend toward pessimism, you are probably glad *someone has come to their senses, as those optimists are a bit irritatingly cheerful anyway.* The pessimist, for your part, will likely feel a resistance during the optimistic part of this exercise. Go ahead and try optimism. Some situations need a bit more hope and positivity.

PERSONAL WORKSHEET

How might you use optimism and pessimism as a
different approach to a current situation?

1. **Think of a situation that could use a bit more optimism.**
   (A situation at home, work, a personal project, friendship,
   that you currently feel a bit resigned or discouraged about
   changing for the better.)

   - What could you say or do that tends toward optimism?
     (Use the *Optimism* chart and your notes from your
     responses as your "personal coach.")
   - What face, tone of voice, or posture might help you to
     enter optimism?

2. **Think of a situation that could benefit from a bit more
   pessimism. (Again, a situation at home, work, a personal
   project, friendship, in which you have been ignoring any
   "negativity" or where you are pretending something is all
   right or tolerable.)**

   - What could you say or do that is aligned with pessimism?
     (Use the *Pessimism* chart and your notes as your "personal
     coach.")
   - What face, tone of voice, or posture might help you to
     enter pessimism?

3. **What did you notice and learn about yourself?**

4. **What, if anything, will you do to change your situation?**

_____

_____

INSIGHTS FROM OTHERS

It never occurred to me that pessimism was a useful emotion and that optimism could be detrimental. During my performance review this week, my boss said he considered me a bit naïve and too cheery, someone who didn't take problems seriously! I thought being cheerful ALWAYS helped people. I left the meeting stunned and am still shell-shocked. Can we talk in our next coaching meeting?

✦

Carol, I think you will appreciate this, as you know I am an over-the-top positivist. Before this exercise, pessimistic people were irritating—plain and simple. I didn't want to hear any of that around me. As you can imagine, the pessimistic task was unwelcome. But I trust you, and so although very skeptical, taking advantage of negativity became my exercise. (Don't you love the irony?)

You would not believe the looks I got in my staff meeting when I asked people to bring up what wouldn't work. There was a long silence. I don't think they believed me. Some said later they thought I was trying to trick them. The best part??? People began to be honest about what they were stuck with, and started to ask for help. I had no idea that too much optimism can grow a culture of looking good at all costs and hiding problems. Yay pessimism.

✦

After reading [fellow student's] account, I, as a dyed-in-the-wool realist (aka pessimist in nice clothes), thought I'd give optimism a try. The best I could do was keep my pessimistic view AND offer ideas or suggestions. I too got weird looks in meetings.

Where to from here?

Hopefully you are beginning to trust yourself and your results from activating emotions, noticing and interrupting your patterns via the activities.

Leave Step 2 when you are ready. Feel free to repeat any exercises or create your own that help you notice and interrupt your patterns associated with self-sacrificing, never enough, and overachieving. Stay long enough to build trust in yourself that you can indeed change even old and long-held undesirable patterns without much effort.

In Step 3 you will actively enter and stay longer in emotions that are the opposite of the self-sacrificing, never-enough, overachieving self.

STEP 3: SAVE YOUR INNER TORTOISE … CROSS FINISH LINES JOYFUL AND SATISFIED

You don't have to change everything for everything to change.

No change of your life's circumstances is required to implement emotional agility. Life does not have to get better before you have a few minutes, hours, or days of relief from a bothersome emotional pattern. Experts in self-sacrificing can indeed take some necessary time away from responsibilities. Overwhelmed overachievers can find replenishment. Someone who is confounded with feelings of insufficiency can feel true satisfaction. Experiencing less and less guilt is also possible. What these "vacations" from our patterns offer is space for rethinking. It is in that space that the origins of new patterns take hold. The more space and time spent, the more your inner tortoise will shape your preferred self.

As we had a glimpse of with the previous opposites activities, patterns can be changed. With a bit of attention and consistency, more constructive patterns are available to you. You do not have to change professions, jobs, projects, or friends to experience life a bit differently. "They" (a child, spouse, ex-spouse, parent, significant other, colleague, or boss) do *not* have to do anything differently for *you* to be a bit more satisfied. Joy is also available.

Best of all? There is no waiting period. You do not have to lose weight, gain weight, or have a different landlord or tenant. Willingness is all you need. A bit of curiosity might make it fun … however, that is not required. Emotional agility works—whether you follow the directions with ease or begrudgingly.

The focus of Step 3 is sustainability of more desirous ways of being and doing. You will actively reshape what you do and how you go about doing it. Instead of spending short time periods in activities, like those in Step 2, you will spend more time in a particular emotion—long enough to see the lingering effects of new patterns. At some point emotions that differ from your old patterns will arise naturally without your having to work hard.

Ready?

> *Author's Story…* Early on in the design of this emotional agility process, I truly hoped there was a "happily ever after" fairy-tale solution for my own and my clients' woes. I was looking for the "Holy Grail." I wanted one answer—now. I had been working hard for a very long time and I was at my wits' end and tired from all the

efforts. I was plenty good at punishing myself for not making it yet. I had not realized I never said what "yet" was. The end was always a moving target. If I had reached it, obviously it wasn't good enough. I was desperate for relief. Wasn't there *one* answer right *now*?

I am sorry to dash any similar hopes of yours.

Although simple, this process is not always easy. I invented the term *Universal Emotions of Well-being* when I realized emotional agility is a skill to develop over time, and not an event. It is a journey with bursts of aliveness over time. Our old self is a strong competitor of the new self we are putting in place. The pull (even logic) of doing what we have been doing is strong. As seen earlier, *aha* moments about our patterns can come from reading and doing simple activities, reading about others' insights, or switching our watch from one arm to another. To some extent, change can happen quickly.

However, some of us have lived the same overwhelming and exhausting patterns for years—maybe decades. What about resolving some of these long-standing fatiguing patterns?

Carol's Coaching Corner: Simply said, undoing years of injurious behaviors and emotions requires practicing more constructive emotions consistently over time. So if you are willing to do the simple work and stick with it, you will reap the rewards.

If you find Step 3 a bit much for you, go back to Step 2 and enjoy those kinds of breaks. **Pattern breaking is pattern breaking.** NO striving for harder is needed. **Repetition is key, not the level of difficulty or effort.**

Thankfully, it does not have to take decades to unravel old patterns.

Let's look at what happens if you have a 1- to 2-minute DAILY gratitude habit. Here's what has been scientifically measured:

> According to research at the Institute of HeartMath, true feelings of gratitude, appreciation and other positive

emotions can synchronize brain and heart rhythms, creating a bodywide shift to a scientifically measurable state called coherence. In this optimal state, the body's systems function more efficiently, generating a greater balance of emotions and increased mental clarity and brain function.

The exercise of activating a positive feeling like appreciation literally shifts our physiology, helping to balance our heart rhythms and nervous system, and creates more coherence between the heart, brain and rest of the body.

- **Biochemical changes** – Favorable changes in the body's biochemistry include improved hormonal balance and an increase in production of DHEA, the "anti-aging hormone."
- **Increased positivity** – Daily gratitude exercises can bring about a greater level of positive feelings, according to researchers from the University of Miami and the University of California, Davis, who studied this process in 157 individuals over 13 days.
- **Boost to the immune system** – The IgA antibody, which serves as the first line of defense against pathogens, increases in the body. [8]
- **Emotional "compound interest"** – The accumulated effect of sustained appreciation and gratitude is that these feelings, and coherence, are easier to recreate with continued practice. This is because experiencing an emotion reinforces the neural pathways of that particular emotion as it excites the brain, heart and nervous system.

Gratitude is a simple and effective practice, and the benefits are real and attainable, and we know this thanks to modern science. Gratitude creates a healthier, happier, and more fulfilling state of being for anyone who takes a few moments to feel and reflect on it. **All in one or two minutes a day!** We don't need science to tell us that gratitude has benefits. Intuitively, this makes sense. We feel better when we appreciate others or when others appreciate us. Our well-being expands when we are satisfied with our efforts, do something wholeheartedly, and feel joy.

Carol's Coaching Corner: Our brain is an equal-opportunity employer! We also can reinforce negative emotions. WE ARE WHAT WE PRACTICE. What are you practicing these days? What are you keeping in motion at home, at work, with yourself?

Remember this illustration? In Step 3 you will be spending your time on the left-hand side of the closet.

THE UNIVERSAL EMOTIONS OF WELL-BEING: JOY, SATISFACTION, AND WHOLEHEARTEDNESS

Human beings are not born once and for all on the day their mothers give birth to them; life obliges them over and over again to give birth to themselves.
~ Gabriel Garcia Marquez

Thankfully, because of our capacity for neural plasticity, we are not condemned to repeat being who we have been in life. Learning emotional agility gives birth to and cultivates new ways of being, doing, and feeling. All that is needed is a desire to change and a willingness to act on it. As with a 1- to 2-minute daily gratitude practice, there are other ways in which you will be visiting satisfaction, wholeheartedness, and joy.

With clients or students, I initially notice two trends: 1) Something in life is off balance. They are aware of something they no longer want in life. 2) They do not connect their disenchantment with life to their emotional patterns and skills. No surprise, since most of us never had that class in Emotions 101. We may have read about Daniel Goleman's *Emotional Intelligence* research but are left with the question of how we get some of that intelligence. As we saw in Steps 1 and 2, what we wear regularly from our emotional wardrobe influences what we say and do … and do not say and do not do. Our emotional patterns directly influence the quality of our life experience. Getting to the *how* is our task in Step 3.

Why this trio of Universal Emotions of Well-being?

Nothing earth shattering here. My clients and students and I simply found them to be antidotes that neutralized the effects of unpleasing emotional patterns that stem from recurrent self-sacrificing, never-enough, over-achieving ways. (If you've forgotten what these "ways" are, return to the checklist on page xvi.)

Emotional Antidotes: An antidote is a medicine or other remedy for counteracting the effects of a poison or disease. In *Destructive Emotions*, the Dalai Lama speaks about a Buddhist belief that there are 10,000 destructive emotions. My first reaction was "we are doomed" with 10,000 negative states! (Not to mention that most of Ekman's universal behavioral essences could be interpreted as "negative": anger, contempt, sadness, fear, and disgust, with surprise and happiness the only "positive" emotions. And some surprises are not that welcome!) However, the Buddhists also believe in antidotes to these "mental afflictions." Matthieu Ricard offers these suggestions for antidotes:

> There is a specific antidote for each emotion. As I mentioned earlier we cannot feel hatred and love simultaneously for the same object. Thus love is a direct antidote to hatred. … For ignorance, or lack of discernment, we try to refine our understanding of what needs to be accomplished and what avoided. In the case of jealousy, one can try to rejoice in others' qualities. For pride, we try to appreciate others'

achievements and open our eyes to our own defects to cultivate humility. [9]

Carol's Coaching Corner: Emotional antidotes like fun, joy, gratitude, lightness, wholeheartedness, and satisfaction counteract the unwanted effects of emotions like resentment, resignation, overwhelm, sadness, regret, despair, self-doubt, or disillusionment. By trying on an emotional antidote, solutions to a problem appear. Sometimes, in the new emotion, the problem disappears with very little effort on our part.

For example: In a flash, while reading about antidotes, I went from anxiety and worry (10,000 destructive emotions) to optimism with the possibility of 10,000 constructive emotions. So many positive states to play with!

Watch for your shifts!

ACTIVATE AND WEAR JOY

Joy has its own structure of accessibility and is not an elusive concept. It can be activated in the simplest of ways. Neuroscientist Gabrielle Leblanc offers:

> Fortunately, changes don't have to be big ones to tip the joy in your favor. David Schkade, PhD, says that if you transfer even an hour of your day from an activity you hate (commuting, scrubbing the bathroom) to one you like (reading, spending time with friends), you should see a significant improvement in your overall happiness. Taking action is key. Another recent study, at the University of Missouri, compared college students who made intentional changes (joining a club, upgrading their study habits) with others who passively experienced positive turns in their circumstances (receiving a scholarship, being relieved of a bad roommate). All the students were happier in the short

term, but only the group who made deliberate changes stayed that way. [10]

As the quote says, *taking action is key.* Adding joy to your emotional wardrobe is about making deliberate changes for immediate benefit. In the following pages you'll find a lot of ideas to bring more joy to your life. *En-joy!*

Joy relieves suffering—plain and simple. For us ever-striving yet never-enough club members and others familiar with life's darker side, it may surprise you that joy is a part of who we are as human beings. Neuropsychologist Richard Hanson, PhD, says joy can be activated by intentional acts:

> The innate neurological circuitry of your mind poses a very real challenge: positive stimuli tend to roll through it while negative stimuli get flagged and captured and deferred to.
>
> But you can consciously override those tendencies in simple and effective ways each day, by focusing on positive experiences, valuing them, and helping them sink in. That's a deeply wise and wonderful undertaking: happiness is skillful means. And happily for happiness, this is aligned with your deepest nature: awake, interested, benign, at peace, and quietly inclined to joy. [11]

Directions: Do a Simple Joy Practice at least once a day for two weeks.

- Following are five ideas. You may choose the same one for two weeks or make a choice each day.

Carol's Coaching Corner: Practice long enough and often enough to feel a sustainable and overall sense of ease with joy. Incorporate into your day instead of feeling like you are adding something to your TO-DO list.

SIMPLE JOY PRACTICE #1

Do something fun each day!

Do something you enjoy at least once a day. And ... you guessed it—enjoy it. Do not allow guilt to take over. (Remember the "itty bitty bitchy committee"? Retire them for this activity!)

- Play a game—not necessarily to win, but to be playful.
- Enjoy a hobby (gardening, crafts, home projects, tinkering)
- Relax with a favorite book.
- Do nothing for 10 or 15 minutes and enjoy it.
- Do something at work that you enjoy.
- Do you know a toddler or child with a wild imagination? Put them in charge of having fun and do what they say.

Personal Reflections

_____

_____

_____

_____

Carol's Coaching Corner: Feel weird, silly, out of sorts, uncomfortable? **Feeling different is a very good sign!** By doing something different, those new neural pathways are altering your physiology as you intentionally bring forth something fun or joyful.

Instead of avoiding these reactions, embrace them. You are noticing emotional agility in action.

SIMPLE JOY PRACTICE #2
Bring joy to others

Take your joy-practicing out into the world of friends, colleagues, storekeepers, co-workers, clients, and vendors.

Actively practice bringing joy to others. Like magic, offering kindness (without expectations) not only brings joy to others, but it generates a feeling of well-being in you.

The trick? Be gracious and generous. Expect nothing in return!

- Say hello with a smile.
- Acknowledge someone you know. (Even if you are busy, busy, busy.)
- Thank people for *any* gesture of kindness. (Their letting you in front of them in a line, opening a door for you, offering to carry your groceries.)
- If you see someone being impatient or having a bad day, let them go first at the post office, grocery store, or while shopping.
- Help someone who is lost or disoriented.
- Instead of averting your eyes, give a smile to a homeless person without judgment or aversion.
- Add an extra scoop of ice cream! (Without guilt!)
- Give a hug.
- Say something kind.

Personal Reflections

_____

_____

_____

_____

SIMPLE JOY PRACTICE #3
Joy Journal

If you like writing, create a comfortable setting for yourself to sit and write about joy. What are you truly grateful for? What delights you? What makes you smile? Feel tenderhearted?

- Write for five minutes. Make it a Joy Journal that you add to every day for two weeks.
- Reread what you wrote, and take a few moments each time to feel gratitude and joy.

HINT: What facial expression and body posture helps you enter joy? (A small smile? Open shoulders to let your heart have some room to open? Extend your spine so that you are sitting or standing more upright instead of being hunched over.)

Personal Reflections

_____

_____

_____

_____

INSIGHTS FROM OTHERS

I can still remember the day Carol took a frustrated, impatient 20-something and gave her the homework assignment of the century. **She requested that I write in a Joy Journal ten moments of joy in every day.** Ten moments of joy… **TEN?!**

I thought perhaps Carol did not fully understand my situation. At the time, I could not see joy in my life. Didn't she know that I was generally lost and unhappy? I had certainly told her enough about the really hard times. I was certainly no candidate for such an outrageous task!

The nerve of her, I thought! With deep resentment, resistance, and certainty of failure, I begrudgingly accepted my homework and went out into my life to look for joy. Surprisingly, things started out rather well....

Joy Journal 3/7

- *Chased my cat Lucky*
- *My boyfriend called early at 6:30*
- *Saw the bougainvilleas in bloom*
- *Watched "Friends" as I worked out and laughed*

Joy Journal 3/8

- *Watched Britney Spears movie with Sue*
- *Sang to Alanis in the car*
- *Received 3 messages*
- *Listened to the band at Beloes*
- *Found out there was karaoke at the dance bar. Singing karaoke.*

But I had some rough days...

Joy Journal 3/9

None—in a bummy mood all day—could not get out of it—identified it as PMS

And I had some days where joy totally slipped my mind

Joy Journal 3/11

None—too busy for joy

And sometimes joy seemed a complete impossibility!

Joy Journal 3/12

Day isn't starting off too well—woke up hating the world with a ton of negative assessments about myself and my relationship as well—keep telling myself to stop and be quiet.

But with practice, little by little, the joy kept coming and my daily list kept growing and growing.

Joy Journal 3/14—Joy! Joy! Joy!

- *Woke up at 5:00 a.m. well-rested and chose to stay in bed until 6:30!!*
- *Enjoyed my friends at the Chamber meeting.*
- *Saw my staff member outside on a break. I gave her a small gesture of appreciation on the way by.*
- *Was asked to chair the next association conference!*
- *Received a $500 donation to the charity because I spoke up!*
- *Scheduled a lunch meeting with J. T.—so exciting!*
- *Came up with the "Work a Mile Program"!!!*
- *My boyfriend invited me for Sushi!*
- *He offered that we could go see the band that I was going to audition for!!*
- *Sang on the way to the manager's meeting.*

Nice day! I was starting to really get the hang of this joy thing!

One of my most memorable breakthroughs on my quest for joy came on a particularly sunny Saturday at a local coffee shop. I had settled in for the afternoon, reading, sipping coffee, munching on chocolate-covered espresso beans, and soaking up the sun. Suddenly, I was struck by the essence of joy so fully and so powerfully that it left me sobbing at the table. I became present to a deep appreciation and a love for the world and for myself within it. I was in awe of the level of joy I was capable of, not just when I was doing "exciting" or "fun" things, but just sitting in a room in the sunshine. With tears still streaming down my face, I called my mother to share the news. I had become a joyful person.

Today, joy comes easily. And thanks to Carol's intervention, I know that joy is not a place to get to, nor is it attached to some thing or person, but instead it is something we can choose to see the world through and something which can be called forth at any moment.

Carpe Diem — Seize the day; great joy waits!

SIMPLE JOY PRACTICE #4

Awakening silent joy

Enjoy Nature!

Go outside or look out a window full of flora (and fauna if you are lucky).

- As in the illustration, stand with your feet apart, arms open, up and out.
- Gaze up and out. Adjust your posture to feel balanced and open.
- Mentally scan your body from head to toe and loosen any tensions (face, jaw, neck, shoulders).
- Soften your eyes (Make them a bit out of focus). Make a slight smile.
- Take slow, even, deep breaths.

Let the strength of Mother Nature take on any stresses and worries.

- **Before you return to the day, say "thank you" three times. (If it helps you, say thank you to life or Mother Nature or yourself.)** (Do not rush. Take a deep breath before and after each thank you. Say it until you mean it.)

Personal Reflections

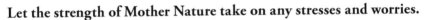

SIMPLE JOY PRACTICE #5
Joyful walking

Take a meandering walk with an intention to feel joy.

- Walk slowly, aimlessly, and without a fixed end or route.
- Allow your head to look up, down, and around.
- Find beauty in whatever surrounds you. Let joy come to you. Turn every once in a while and move in a new direction.
- Let your arms swing. Breathe in and out through your nose. Lower your shoulders.
- At the end of the walk, say "Thank you" to life three times.

Personal Reflections

_____

_____

_____

_____

INSIGHTS FROM OTHERS

Since I love cooking, this came to me this morning.

My Recipe for Success: Creating Lightness and Joy Daily

- Add a pinch of irreverence
- A heaping cup of meaningful work
- A gallon of perfect health, well-being, and flexibility
- Three loving relationships that support and sustain who I am
- At least one teaspoon of creative thought
- Mix lightly with joyful music and cook with tender care at a moderate pace, remembering to relax and do nothing for at least 10 minutes a day!

♦

Carol, I thought you'd enjoy that others around the world are getting on the fun bandwagon with you as an antidote to worry, skepticism, and cynicism. *http://www.thefuntheory.com/* "This site is dedicated to the thought that something as simple as fun is the easiest way to change people's behavior for the better. Be it for yourself, for the environment, or for something entirely different, the only thing that matters is that it is change for the better."

♦

It took some time to "be" joyful. I kept thinking of all the things that were wrong in my life. Mimicking the drawing of joy was the trick for me. (I just couldn't be bitchy with my arms open wide and a smile on my face! I'd start to laugh at myself.)

For me, joy was not an over-the-top emotion as I expected. Instead of brimming with joy, it brought me a calm or deep sense of wonder and awe. (Several times I had tears well up—tears of joy.) "Sweet" is a word that comes to mind.

♦

I've been practicing by enlarging my appreciation and acceptance. One day, JOY showed up! It's a moment I'll treasure forever. And relive often. Also, the more I practice, the more I see that Peace and Grace are mighty fine as preferred emotions, not just transitional ones. It seems that Joy is kind of a given once I've made it into Peace and Grace.

Author's Story... **From my 2009 Joy notes.** For me personally, along with their emotional cousin of lightness, gratitude and joy are proving to be *the* way out of my much-practiced, well-embodied resignation, incessant regretting, and fired-up resentment.

I am years into this personal lightness/joy agenda and still—you guessed it—enjoying it. I can depend on my agility for a quick visit to joy to relieve suffering. These days joy often arrives unheralded. I find myself smiling at the trees or sky. On the way to the grocery store, a smile will wash over me for no apparent reason. I have learned to enjoy those moments.

What is surprising is that I tend not to panic with onsets of anger, resentment, and frustration. With gratitude and joy as a balancing force, I don't seem to fear the darkness as much. "This too shall pass" is my mantra. The other day I was really down on myself. Back to my "you are no good and never will be." Instead of trying to "fix it" with one of my many practices, I decided instead to really get into "Beulah"—the name I'd given this super critical side of me. So I left the office, bought some chocolate, and turned on Oprah. I had a fabulous pity party for an hour. Tears. Chocolate. Seeing others who were also suffering. I am really good at self-pity.

At the end, when I turned off the TV, the negativity was "off" too.

ACTIVATE AND WEAR SATISFACTION

Author's Story… My passion for satisfaction!

My true passion for this emotional state comes from the breath of fresh air that interrupted a pattern of living that had gone too far down a detrimental path. Satisfaction saved me from myself. Lest I seem a bit dramatic … you be the judge:

From grade school to my early 40s I was a world-class pleaser. I wanted everyone to like me and approve of me. I always said yes—even when I wanted to or should have said no. Employers loved me. I'd arrive early, stay late, and pick up the slack of others. A pat on the back or a thank you went a long way to ensure more of this indulging others. All this pleasing fueled my ambition. And just in case I got tired, my extra boost was guilt with "shoulds" that came from dreading disappointing others.

Over time my norm became that nothing was ever enough. Perfectionism was my middle name. My Martha Stewart™ tendencies extended beyond home and cooking to work projects. There was always more that could be done—without ever asking if more was desired. The final part of this pattern was the second-guessing AFTER completion. Something always could have been done better. I criticized all completed tasks in some fashion. (I was disheartened when 1 percent of training feedback forms revealed disappointment with the class. I readily dismissed the other 99 percent positive ones.)

Stress, overwhelm, and rushing about to get everything done on time. Busy every minute. My lunch of choice was a big, strong mug of coffee at my desk. After hours, weekends, and vacations were times to catch up on work. I followed the motto: Under-promise and over-deliver. (However, I wasn't so good at the under-promising part. That's the problem with always saying yes. People keep asking for more.)

I hear some of you screaming "JUST SAY NO!" Well, I thought of that too. However, ANY consideration of saying no or asking for help was like a whisper. Guilt kicked in immediately and the "no" disappeared.

Don't get me wrong. I was proud of my successes and there were benefits to all this hard work. My pride soared with being trusted as a go-to person for challenging projects. Raises, bonuses, awards, public acknowledgments, promotions, and titles like director and vice president were like puffs of fresh air. Saying no seemed like a dumb idea.

So what's the problem? To be honest, getting older, disenchantment, and rising resentment were the problem. After 40+ years of this, I was exhausted. "Is this all there is?" began seeping into my consciousness.

Satisfaction was my doorway out.

Carol's Coaching Corner: Sometimes I feel a bit un-American when I propose being satisfied as a Universal Emotion of Well-being. Some might construe it as working against our culture of ever-striving. The #1 rule of ever-striving is ... MORE—MORE—MORE! What seems truly ironic is that all the rewards and benefits of this hard work are, in the end, NOT enough. We barely stop to enjoy the fruits of our labors before we are on to the next task. Can exhaustion and disillusionment be far behind?

So forgive me for interrupting our world of wanting, needing, and excessive doing, for some rest and replenishment. As my cure to overdoing on pleasing, satisfaction opens us to peace of mind and a renewed sense of energy.

Don't worry ... striving and "not enough" will be there waiting for you when necessary or useful. We are merely adding an emotion to your wardrobe.

You are in the right place if you wish to have a vacation from ever-striving, overwhelm, fear, anxiety, not being or feeling enough, self-doubt, or lack of self-confidence. Why? Satisfaction is the emotion of setting boundaries.

What is satisfaction?

The origins of the word *satisfaction* will help us understand a critical component for satisfaction—setting boundaries or limits.

Satisfacere: *satis* (enough) + *facere* (to make, to do). Enough doing! Enough action.

Emotional Cousins (related emotions): feeling compensated, contented, convinced, filled, fulfilled, gratified, happy, positive, quenched, sated, satiated.

Let's go a bit further with "enough." Definitions of *enough* are: *sufficient for the purpose; to satisfy a desire; answers a purpose; suffices for now.*

The language of enough: abundant, acceptable, adequate, all right, ample, bellyful, bountiful, comfortable, competent, complete, copious, decent, enough already, fed up, full, had it, just right, the last straw, plentiful, replete, sick and tired of, sufficient, sufficing, suitable.

For some of us, it has been awhile since we truly visited satisfaction. If you have *ever* felt satisfied, this is an emotional recovery process. So dust yourself off and jump in.

The core question ... What IS enough?

Author's Story... My first week of practicing satisfaction had me feeling nauseated after a minute or two. I was fascinated by my expertise at self-doubting and especially criticizing anything and everything. I always compared myself unfavorably with others who were better. In the first few days, NOTHING was enough. Wow ... was I THAT far gone? Apparently so. The good news was that I got sick and tired of myself.

Carol's Coaching Corner: Measure of success? Increasing the time you can spend being satisfied. (If you start at one minute, then two minutes is a 100 percent improvement.) Remember, the goal is being satisfied. Poet David Whyte says, "Arrange to get tired of yourself." Arrange to get tired of your dissatisfaction habit. You **must** be willing to leave your not-enough patterns to be satisfied. Give it a good try. See if you like how life is with satisfaction. (You can always go back to insufficiency.)

Activate Satisfaction: The following activities allow you to enter dissatisfaction as well as satisfaction briefly.

AWARENESS ACTIVITY

How do you know you might need or want satisfaction?

Attitudes or ways of being that move you *away from* being satisfied.

Excessive eagerness. A general sense of urgency in life.

Controlling. (You cannot let things or people be as they are.)

Always rushing or feeling rushed.

Chronic lateness. Feeling pushed or pulled forward.

Ever striving. Feeling overwhelmed. Impatience.

Multitasking, yet never done. Just one more thing.

Personal Reflections

What do you do to move away from satisfaction?

_____

_____

_____

_____

_____

AWARENESS ACTIVITY

What attitudes and behaviors keep us in dissatisfaction?

Do you know fear, anxiety, dread, or fretting well?

Do you have a "worrying habit"? Are you an "awful-izer"? (In minutes, the future is awful!)

Do you persistently regret what did or did not happen in the past?

Are you generally anxious about the future?

Does your worry lead you to more worry?

Greed ... Always want more. **Scarcity ...** There's never enough. **Hoarding ...** I have to hold on and keep.

Do you tend to be at war with anything and everything?

Persistent disagreeing? Cranky? Grumpy?

Chronic second-guessing? Doubt? Self-Doubt?

Do you surround yourself with critical people?

Do they find you?

Personal Reflections

What are your dissatisfaction patterns?

_____

_____

_____

_____

AWARENESS ACTIVITY

What attitudes and behaviors activate and sustain satisfaction?

Being calm, calmer, or calming.

At peace with…   Make peace with…

Slow down…   Slowing…   A bit slower pace…   Practicing patience

Adjust your breathing pattern to slow and even breaths.

Effective worry (that results in corrective action).

Economy of action (the least amount of effort to complete).

Taking a break (long enough to feel a bit refreshed and replenished).

Forgiveness (of self and others).

Allowance.

Graciousness.

What are your favorite five?

- _____
- _____
- _____
- _____
- _____

SIMPLE SATISFACTION PRACTICE

Practice your favorite five

Like multiple vitamins, practice one of your five each day until you are satisfied.

- YOU are the one who determines when you are satisfied.
- Take care not to employ your old never-enough standards.
- Remember, the goal of satisfaction is determining "What is enough?"

Personal Reflections

_____

_____

_____

_____

_____

SIMPLE SATISFACTION PRACTICE
Take a bath or shower* for pleasure

- As you draw the bath or prepare for the shower, pay attention to what will make it a lovely experience: water temperature, possible beverage, candles, music, bubbles, body wash, privacy and quiet.
- Enjoy!
- If you find yourself ruminating about the past or thinking about the future, splash yourself in the face and get back to enjoying.
- Closing your eyes and frequently sighing with satisfaction help!

Also consider taking pleasure in whatever task you are doing! A walk. A work project. Gardening. A hobby. Taking out the garbage.

Personal Reflections

_____

_____

_____

_____

_____

Wearing Satisfaction:

In these activities, you will extend the amount of time and the places where you wear satisfaction. The ultimate aim of these extended practices is that you begin to experience the emotion of satisfaction over longer periods and in different situations. At some point you will begin to crave or feel the urge to stop overdoing, and you'll do just that. As you learn "enough," you will set boundaries.

The goal is enjoying the pleasure of adequacy for your wants or needs instead of feeling insufficiency.

Let these words from poet and international speaker David Whyte inspire you:

Enough

Enough. These few words are enough.
If not these words, this breath.
If not this breath, this sitting here.
This opening to the life
we have refused
again and again
until now.
Until now.

In this moment of epiphany

This opening to the life
we have refused
again and again
until now. [12]

The language of satisfaction

As we saw in Step 2, our emotions have patterns. An important entry point into any emotion is what we say and how we say it. Language is generative. We become as we speak. What we say brings forth our future. Trying on satisfaction requires a specific language.

Declarations of completion or ending:

Enough!   Enough already!   Stop!   Stop it!

I am finished.   I am happy with...   I am happy.

I am satisfied that...   I am satisfied.   I am content.

I am done with...   I will no longer...

Thank you.   Yes, thank you.   No, thank you.

How satisfaction works when there is more to be done:

Enough for now.   I am finished for now.

I am setting this aside until... [time and date]

Acceptance:

I accept that this will happen.   I accept that this will not happen.

SIMPLE SATISFACTION PRACTICE
Use the language of satisfaction

1. Use the language of satisfaction at least *five times a day* for two weeks.

2. At the end of the day, recall your moments of satisfaction.

3. Do a "happy dance"* before you go to bed.

*A "happy dance" is your version of dancing or moving around while being pleased with keeping your promise to be satisfied. Do NOT skip this step.

Personal Reflections

_____

_____

_____

_____

SIMPLE SATISFACTION PRACTICE
A satisfaction journal

1. At the end of every day, write down in a journal or log exactly what you are satisfied with.

2. After writing, take a few moments to enjoy the satisfaction. (Do not skip this step!)
   - Be specific and sense satisfaction fully in your body.

Carol's Coaching Corner: Watch out for thinking something is too small or menial to "count" toward satisfaction. If at *some* level you were pleased, happy, satisfied, delighted, or okay with ... WRITE IT DOWN. Take care *not* to add any language that takes away from your satisfaction. (Should, should have, could, could have, if only, if I would have.)

Personal Reflections

_____

_____

_____

_____

_____

SIMPLE SATISFACTION PRACTICE
Take a meandering walk* or hike in nature

- Go to a favorite spot outside.
- Find a new one!
- Take a walk in the sun, rain, or snow.
- Be aware and conscious of your surroundings.
- Take full and slow breaths.
- When distracted, return to noticing you are in nature.
- Pause, wander, stop a few times along the way.

No intense calorie-burning exercise this time around. This is a relaxing stroll.

Personal Reflections

_____

_____

_____

_____

_____

SIMPLE SATISFACTION PRACTICE
Saying yes or no

Only two rules:

1. Say yes when you mean yes. Say no when you mean no.

2. Keep your promises.

YES

Yes = I promise to do *x* by time *y*.

No

No thank you.   Not today.   Not until … [time and date]

A "no" is a promise NOT to.

I promise not to do that today.

I will reconsider on x date.

Personal Reflections

_____

_____

_____

_____

_____

> **Carol's Coaching Corner:** A few words about tone of voice...
>
> Your tone of voice will make a big difference in your level of satisfaction and that of others. Does a loud and booming voice produce the results you want? On the other hand, does calmness and a voice loud enough to be heard produce the results you want?
>
> You can scream "no" or you can say "no" with a quiet and deliberate conviction. Which cultivates satisfaction in you and others? (This assumes you care that others are also satisfied, which may or may not be the case for you.)

INSIGHTS FROM OTHERS

My version of satisfaction became saying "I get to." That seemed to get me to happiness/enjoyment/a more satisfied mood, vs. saying "I have to," which feels like obligation/crankiness/dissatisfaction waiting to happen.

I notice a difference in my energy level when I'm in the "I have to" mode vs. the "I get to" mode. My body feels physically different.

✦

I learned very well how to make critical judgments. I did not learn well the move of declaring satisfaction.

✦

In a mood of satisfaction, I am more open to offers and requests.

✦

In class today you mentioned your mom saying "any decent daughter would know what I want ... I shouldn't have to tell you." Your story revealed [that] I thought the same in my family. *I think any decent son or wife SHOULD do what I want.* My unexpected insight was that I am a chronic "should-er" at home. I try to guilt people into doing chores (Somebody else in this family should clean the garage. Why am I the only one who does the dishes? Doesn't anybody else care but me?) I realized I do not make requests. I expect. I never ask my son or wife specifically—they should know better.

Now I ask more often, and am happy to report there is more peace at home. I don't scream much at all anymore. I am waiting for the day someone volunteers to do a chore. However, in the meantime, I ask.

✦

I'm really more prone to dissatisfaction and getting more so. I really am a cranky person at home, at work, and even in the line at the grocery store. I am happy to report a growing dissatisfaction with my dissatisfaction.

✦

More people are saying hi and/or stopping to have a conversation with me when I am walking down the street or at my desk.

✦

My daughter is hugging me lots, and she hasn't done that for a long time. (Is it coincidental with my satisfaction practice?)

SIMPLE SATISFACTION PRACTICE

Satiation—"What is enough" food or drink?

- Actually *taste* and *enjoy* what you eat and drink!
- Pause between bites and sips. Savor!
- Keep breathing.
- Eat and drink slowly enough to recognize satiation—enough food and drink.
- Stop when you are full or are approaching enough. (It may come much faster than you think.)
- Declare satisfaction. (Use the language of satisfaction.)
- Make a ritual or ceremony of putting the food and drink away.

Personal Reflections

_____

_____

_____

_____

_____

INSIGHTS FROM OTHERS

The first thing I noticed is that sometimes nothing would satisfy me. I wasn't eating because I was hungry—I was just eating to fill a void that food wouldn't fill. So I always ate past full. One trick was to stop at the first hint of satiation and wait 20 minutes. Often I was no longer hungry.

At first I saved it for later. However, saving it seemed to keep the craving going for some reason. Then I did the ceremony part as you suggested. Throwing food away was freeing. I paid attention to throwing food away and NOT saving it for later. (Remember my mother rolling over in her grave? I am pretty sure she's doing it again with me throwing away food.)

Satiation for me was more of a releasing exercise. I like feeling free. My new mantra: I am free to eat later.

✦

My doctor told me that my growling stomach may be thirst, not hunger for food. I now drink water first and see what happens.

✦

My *aha* moment was to eat when I was hungry and not when it was lunch or dinner "time."

Other Satisfaction Practice Ideas from Students

Using movement:

- Combined with some of my tai chi moves, I've been saying aloud "I am satisfied." I play around with the tone of my voice and practice having the tone come from the chi center, just below the belly button.
- I frequently put a slight smile on my face. It is a great intervention just by itself. The smile is slight, not one of full-on happy.
- I have been walking in dissatisfaction. It is like I am "dissatisfaction just waiting to happen." Now I am moving to walking in satisfaction and satisfaction waiting to happen.
- I try a goooooooooood stretch every hour. (I set a recurring reminder for the first few days on my computer until I did it automatically.)

Using voice:

- Singing and humming my revised version of the Rolling Stones' song "Satisfaction." (I can get lots … of satisfaction.) I do this throughout the day, on the way to work, climbing the stairs, riding on the bus, walking to/from the bus stop.
- Sometimes I play with the way I walk while singing or humming. For example, I add a bounce to my step. The satisfaction walk includes head held high, looking about and taking in the surroundings, chest open with slight smile and eyes wide open.

- My kids do what I ask if I don't whine. Seems so obvious now, and it wasn't before.

At work:

- I push back in my chair, open up my chest, smile and breathe deeply, and exhale with a sigh of satisfaction.
- My satisfaction options: re-choose or un-choose or renegotiate.
- Before and during meetings for which I anticipate I will need my "Teflon coating," I start humming a song to myself while on the phone with my counterpart at another location. She's one of the best people for me to practice with, because her emotions are powerful and they aren't the ones I want for myself.
- I take wellness breaks. I am in a room full of people working on a big proposal. It's fun, noisy, and intense. I go on a cruise around the room and give a good stretch and a satisfaction sigh and say "nice work" to myself and to colleagues. Some of us take stretch breaks at the same time without planning it.
- I am getting a slow start on my daily practices due to some really BIG commitments through this week. I am noticing, though, that when I bring my awareness to my current mood and shift toward satisfaction that I usually succeed. Very cool.

Carol's Coaching Corner: I leave you with these thoughts on satisfaction: Go for emotional agility ... NOT emotional perfection!

Finish every day and be done with it.
You have done what you could.

Some blunders and absurdities no doubt have
crept in; forget them as soon as you can.

Tomorrow is a new day; begin it well and
serenely and with too high a spirit to be
cumbered with your old nonsense.

This day is all that is good and fair.
It is too dear, with its hopes and invitations,
to waste a moment on yesterdays.
- Ralph Waldo Emerson

ACTIVATE AND WEAR WHOLEHEARTEDNESS

Again I turn to poet David Whyte, who offers an insight into what is missing when much of our life includes overwhelm and exhaustion. He says we lack the capacity for being wholehearted:

"The antidote to exhaustion is wholeheartedness."

He looked at me for a *wholehearted* moment, as if I should fill in the blanks. But I was a blank to be filled at that moment, and though I knew something pivotal had been said, I had not the wherewithal to say anything in reply. So he carried on:

"You are so tired through and through because a good half of what you do here in this organization has nothing to do with your true powers, or the place you have reached in your life. You are only half here, and half here will kill you after a while. You need something to which you can give your full powers. You know what that is; I don't have to tell you."

He didn't have to tell me. Brother David knew I wanted my work to be my poetry.

"Go on," I said.

"You are like Rilke's Swan in his awkward waddling across the ground; the swan doesn't cure his awkwardness by beating himself on the back, by moving faster, or by trying to organize himself better. He does it by moving toward the elemental water where he belongs. It is the simple contact with the water that gives him grace and presence. You only have to touch the elemental waters in your own life, and it will transform everything. But you have to let yourself down into those waters from the ground on which you stand, and that can be hard. Particularly if you think you might drown." He looked down and read again.

And to die, which is the letting go of the ground we stand on and cling to every day . . .

He looked up again, warming to the theme, I was getting a good talking-to. "This nervously letting yourself down, this *ängst-lichen Sich-Niederlassen,* as it says in the German, takes courage, and the word courage in English comes from the old French word *cuer,* heart. You must do something heartfelt, and you must do it soon. Let go of all this effort, and let yourself down, however awkwardly, into the waters of the work you want for yourself. It's all right, you know, to support yourself with something secondary until your work has ripened, but once it has ripened to a transparent fullness, it has to be gathered in. You have ripened already, and you are waiting to be brought in. Your exhaustion is a form of inner fermentation. You are beginning, ever so slowly," he hesitated, "to rot on the vine." [13]

Are you, as David Whyte suggests, trying to cure your awkwardness by trying to organize yourself better?

With all of our electronic technology to "help" us, multitasking seems to be a necessity. In minutes, those we care about and others we don't even know bombard us with texts, emails, beeps and rings announcing that someone is connecting with us. Our natural reaction is to answer it, just as we would a phone or a doorbell. Even when we're busy with something to finish, it is hard to resist the temptation to look and see who it is. Once we look, the interruption time expands. Requests, offers, demands, or guilt-generating appeals take our attention. Multiply these minutes into a full day's work and the overload is in full gear.

It is it any wonder we are exhausted? The cost? Aliveness. We have become addicted to staying in communication. We feel the weight of responsibilities and yet cannot wade through the information overload to get what we need.

We work harder and not always smarter. We need more hours, more technology tools, more, more, and more! Is your efficiency more of an illusion than reality? Is what is important or what you truly care about lost in the flood of activity?

Our natural reaction to exhaustion has been rest from overdoing. What is interesting about wholeheartedness is that you actually continue to get things done while adopting a new attitude. Trying on wholeheartedness changes *how* you go about doing something and not necessarily *what* you do.

Students and clients report they feel more alive while being wholehearted doing the same day-to-day activities! Whether carving out time to play with their children, finally completing a project, teaming with others on a challenging project, or finally implementing an exercise routine, they have a renewed sense of passion.

As with satisfaction, we continue to interrupt what is normal for patterns of insufficiency. In terms of emotional agility, trying on wholeheartedness allows you to transform ...

From:

- Excessive procrastination
- Avoiding or postponing what is important
- Overwhelm
- Sense of inadequacy
- Anxiety, fretting, and worry

To:

Feeling a renewed sense of aliveness, fulfillment, and peace of mind as you complete day-to-day commitments.

Author's Story... I was reupholstering some dining-room chairs while my husband was watching a program on the Dalai Lama in the next room. I overheard something about inner peace and paying attention to what you are doing as you are doing it. I was doing nothing of the sort. I was fighting with the fabric (*Stupid stripes aren't matching up*), beating up on myself (*What ever possessed you to pick stripes? You aren't good enough.*), wanting a power stapler instead of the manual one. (*Why do I NEVER do anything the easy way?*)

No inner peace here.

I overheard one of the Buddhist monks talk about breathing. I took a few deep breaths and slowed myself down. I c-a-r-e-f-u-l-l-y put the staple gun in the spot I wanted and pressed the trigger. I gently pulled the fabric to the next right spot and pulled the trigger again. It felt like magic. I couldn't believe the elegance of working this way. There was a rhythm to my movements—almost effortless matching the stripes. In the end, I had three chairs with stripes a bit off center and five chairs with stripes that matched. (As a practice of acceptance and grace, I decided NOT to go back and re-do the first three. I gave my perfectionism the afternoon off.)

What to expect from wearing wholeheartedness

Feeling completely sincere in your efforts.

Feeling a genuine enthusiasm rather than pretense.

Feeling refreshed and able to stop after a job well done.

♥

Passion.

♥

Confusion or chaos replaced by sureness, steadiness of pace, unwavering consistency.

♥

Being able to do something in earnest—authentically, rather than halfheartedly.

Feeling the sense of energy that comes from being committed to an outcome and steadfast in your execution—without overwhelm.

♥

Simple Practices for Wearing Wholeheartedness

Wholeheartedness is a precious gift, but no one can actually give it to you. You have to find the path that has heart and then walk it impeccably … It's like someone laughing in your ear, challenging you to figure out what to do when you don't know what to do. It humbles you. It opens your heart.
~ Pema Chödrön, The Wisdom of No Escape

DIRECTIONS: The following pages offer several wholehearted activities and practices. Select what you want for yourself. Whatever you choose, follow the instructions!

Carol's Coaching Corner:

- Trust the instructions! Before you start getting too creative, let the strategy behind the instructions serve you well.
- Being alert and aware of how you are going about doing, as you are doing it, is more important than the result.
- Being wholehearted during the time spent on individual tasks is more important than how much time you spend. (Twenty minutes of wholehearted effort is better than two hours of dabbling here and there.)
- If you tend to overdo or consistently push past boundaries, keep to the time limit no matter what!

SIMPLE WHOLEHEARTED PRACTICE
The 20-minute practice

I invented this practice after finding that many of my clients who enjoyed the satisfaction practices had a lot on their plates—as parents, community activists, and leaders in their organizations. Many reported feeling pushed and pulled, distracted, and at the end of the day, feeling that nothing much was accomplished or completed considering what was STILL pending.

How could satisfaction spread to their considerable to-do lists and challenging responsibilities?

Wholeheartedness!

Carol's Coaching Corner: Recommended for those who procrastinate, avoid, second-guess, feel a project is too hard, too complicated, too big, overwhelming, etc.

Rules of the practice:

1. **Do a task for 20 minutes. TOTAL. No more. No less.**

   - Twenty minutes is all you get, whether the "task" is reading, sunbathing, napping, cleaning, organizing, fixing, writing, emailing, thinking, preparing, texting, phoning, or whatever.
   - Set a timer.
   - If need be, begin to wind down and prepare to stop at the five-minute point.

2. **You MUST stop after 20 minutes, even if you are enthusiastic or "on a roll."**

   - Stop even if there is more to do.
   - Stop if there is only a little bit left to do.
   - Do *not* come back a few minutes later to finish up. (If there is more to do, wait at least two hours to return to this task.)

3. **At the end of 20 minutes, use the language of completion.**

   - I am done. I DID what I promised. I have completed my 20 minutes. I am done for this round. I am finished for now and I promise to return [at a later date and time].
   - **Do *not* forget or skip this part.**
   - A promise made and a promise kept can dissolve anxiety, fretting, worry, or second-guessing.

Carol's Coaching Corner: Not quite feeling the level of satisfaction with these wholehearted efforts? Bring the body in to help you:

The completion sigh: As you declare completion, stand or sit up, open your arms and chest. Raise your head, chin up a bit, and put a slight smile on your face. (Smug is okay. No big grin.) Take a deep breath in through your nose and exhale through your mouth with the sound of "ahhhhhh." Do it with a tone of being pleased or satisfied.

Repeat as needed until you are sincere!

Personal Reflections

_____

_____

_____

_____

_____

INSIGHTS FROM OTHERS

When I tried this practice, my internal itty bitty bitchy committee had a field day in the beginning. I heard their voices loud and clear: *I should have done this before. Twenty minutes is not near enough time. There is so much more to do, I can't stop now... I feel silly saying, "I am done" out loud. How can I be satisfied when there's so much more to do?* I was pretty sure the goal of this exercise wasn't the anxiety I was feeling. My trick? Breathing! Instead of a feeling of satisfaction at the end, my fast and shallow breathing was actually creating more anxiety! I added slow deep breaths BEFORE saying "I am done." Worked like a charm.

✦

My *aha* moment was once I got started, realizing how much energy and enthusiasm I had. Why had I been avoiding this? It's actually fun! Stopping became the discipline to develop. (My clue to the importance of stopping? When I did *not* stop—as I said I would—my not being enough came back!)

◆

I actually made $ doing this practice! Background … The right environment makes a BIG difference: I realized that wholeheartedness is *not* possible for bill paying in the middle of the kitchen with kids and dogs around! This was a great teacher for creating a supportive environment for emotional learning and getting my bills paid on time. The right place? The basement storeroom. While not the most glamorous spot, it's big and the kids and dogs don't like it down there. How I'm earning $? No more late fees!

◆

On Friday, I had to work on a RFP for a new client. I am not a procrastinator, I am a perfectionist, so my motto used to be "not good enough," which made me spend more time and energy to write a proposal than was actually required, just adding to my feeling of being overwhelmed. This week it was different. I established I would work wholeheartedly on the proposal for one hour only, would file it as a draft, and the following day would review it for 30 minutes and send it. And it worked! Boy, was I satisfied and proud of my achievement!

◆

My contribution this week is two-fold. The antidote I have been practicing is wholeheartedness. The practices (and perhaps the unspoken support of this group) seemed to make the completion of an article I was writing become doable and even fun. It was still work. The self-monitoring I did was totally different from how it might have been in the past. I did not set a timer, but I did work in smaller segments, becoming aware of when I could not sustain the wholeheartedness and taking a break—listening to some music, experiencing some joy or gratitude, having a little cup of tea, etc. I felt very proud of the completed product and very fulfilled. Thank you.

◆

This has been really useful in service to my satisfaction as well as practice in wholeheartedness: 20 minutes of focused effort on tasks that involve activities that I tend to "not like to do":

- Certain client notes.
- Reading a coaching-related book—right now, *The Alba of Emotions.*
- Cardio exercise—this one has a 30-minute timeframe.
- Balancing the checkbook, writing the bills.
- Cleaning up my email inbox.

SIMPLE WHOLEHEARTED PRACTICE
Touch it once

Overwhelmed? Got a mess on your hands? Gripped by anxiety and don't know where to start?

This is the practice for you!

Arrange to get tired of yourself. ~ David Whyte

The energy that works especially well with this practice is being sick and tired that you have not started or completed something like long lists, messes, or projects of any sort with lots of tasks or parts. Do as David Whyte suggests and arrange to get tired of the "self" that is overwhelmed, guilty, or angry. Honor what you say you want!

Name the project

_____

_____

_____

_____

_____

What does *done* look like? (Nothing in your inbox? A clean desk? An organized workstation? A clean garage with everything put on shelves or in a cabinet? Project tasks finished?)

_____

_____

_____

_____

_____

_____

_____

Two rules:

1. **Set a time limit.**

   - If time runs out and you don't finish, that is okay. You are done for that round!
   - If you finish the pile/project/list and there is still time left, you are done!

2. **Within that time limit, *whatever* you touch, finish it or move it to the next step.**

   - For example, if there is a pile of anything, whatever you touch FIRST in that pile you must decide on and put it where it goes. (In the trash, inbox, outbox, filed away, donation box, delegate to, request to, etc.)
   - Do not add it back to the same pile.

Carol's Coaching Corner: It works whether you are cleaning house, a closet, decluttering your desk, or reorganizing files.

This practice also works for emails, to-do lists, project tasking, or any major undertaking that has multiple tasks.

Personal Reflections

_____

_____

_____

_____

_____

INSIGHTS FROM OTHERS

My office was a mess of papers and unopened boxes from my move (six months ago). You couldn't tell the color of my desk. Carol said that this is MY practice to design, so this may be cheating, but it worked to outsmart my procrastinating demons:

While cleaning off my desk, I found some things I just could not face. I just couldn't bring myself to do THAT now. (AND ... I still had time left on the clock.) My trick was to move the paper by blowing on it until I found something underneath more appealing and touched that. That worked swell until what I was avoiding was the only task left and time had not run out. Being a person who is competitive and who likes to win, I took a few deep breaths and broke *that* task into smaller tasks on pieces of paper. Ta da—Satisfaction! I was very pleased to have killed off some of my perfectionist cells!

✦

This practice left me feeling much more in charge of my life. I felt like a king instead of a slave.

✦

With the "touching it once" exercise, I discovered a cool feature of my Outlook email list: messages with auto preview! Before this tool, all I knew was the sender and subject. Now I get a preview of what it says. I leave the email in my inbox until I am ready to move it forward or finish it. This worked especially well with emails from my boss, when I dreaded hearing from him when I wasn't ready or hadn't done my part of a task yet. I have a suggestion to add: I reminded myself to BREATHE before I clicked/ touched the email. Worked really well.

Twists and Turns on our Emotional Agility Journey

Adding to our emotional wardrobe can take many twists and turns. Truthfully, I would prefer getting from point A to point B to be straightforward, with little effort and FAST!

A=Resentment ➜ B=Lightness

However, emotional learning can be a bit unpredictable and circuitous. In my experience, adding lightness to my wardrobe required that I add seriousness, sincerity, rigor, discerning between rage and anger, gratitude, and forgiveness, to name a few. The journey looked more like this ...

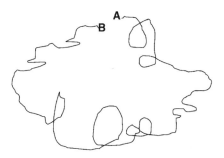

> **Carol's Coaching Corner:** Lest this feel a bit discouraging, let me also offer that accepting this circuitry offers fun and often profound learning experiences along the journey from A to B. Whatever constructive emotion you are adding to your wardrobe may indeed take you to and through many Emotional Cousins—the array of emotions that are related to each other. (Synonyms and antonyms are a good source of possible options for your emotional cousins.)

Author's Story... My own journey from a mood of resentment to one of lightheartedness took many surprising turns. The journey started with embarrassment.

I had taken a new job with my "dream" company and I noticed in my first week that I was "the dark one." My sole contribution at meetings focused on finding who was to blame for the issues and problems we were encountering with a new project. When I stopped to notice, team members around the table had looks of perplexity. At one point, the team leader suggested that "if we have time to find blame we'll do that, but for now let's solve the problems." My face flushed. I felt reprimanded, and I don't like looking bad! Mind you, at my previous employ, finding blame was always on the agenda at meetings. We would look for who was at fault, make it public in a meeting or memo, and then create a procedure to prevent it happening again. I used to call them the "blame and shame" meetings. Frankly, that went against my grain. My practice at my former employ was to bring humor to all this blaming. However, at this new company, their level of lightness was way beyond mine. (That was a large part of why I accepted their job offer.) I had to "up" my lightness level to be a part of this group. Their emotion matched my learning goal of leaving resentment.

The second surprising turn on the way to lightness was learning dignity. In order for me to leave resentment, dignity was an emotion of setting boundaries and being responsible. I saw that blaming others left me faultless. (That seemed like a good strategy if I wanted to look good.) Problem is, if I avoid responsibility and risk (and this avoidance is key to maintaining resentment), I don't get the benefits of responsibility. I saw that true personal pride when getting kudos from others for completing projects or fixing problems came from my being responsible. That was a conundrum for my pleaser ways. As a pleaser, I said yes all of the time and found myself back in resentment. (*Too much to do and it was their fault. They should know I am busy and not ask.*) Sigh! I was good at being blameless. Learning the emotion of dignity required that I be careful what I said yes to. Practicing dignity allowed me to set realistic deadlines and expectations. Over time I could even say no without guilt. Who knew that when you say no to people they could in turn trust your yeses?

Anger was and still is a part of my journey from resentment to lightness. As a "good girl" I typically suppress anger until, like a pressure cooker, I explode. Although still easier said than done, I am learning that anger spoken in the moment of disappointment or frustration relieves pressure and does not foster the lingering resentful predisposition to hold grudges.

SIMPLE WHOLEHEARTED PRACTICE
Design your own

In this activity, you will invent your own wholehearted practice by taking advantage of the many aspects or emotional cousins of wholeheartedness.

- In Column A are the qualities associated with being wholehearted.
- In Column B are familiar tasks, projects, or activities.

Column A: Emotional Cousins of Wholeheartedness	Column B: Task/Project/Activity
Fully or completely sincere	Rest (daydreaming, purposelessness)
Enthusiastic	Learning (reading, classes, workshops)
Energetic	Project/task (work, home, garden, repairs)
In earnest	Housekeeping (dishes, closet, desk, cleaning up rooms)
Serious (intention or intensity)	Hobbies
Passionate	Exercise (sports, or fitness)
Sure, with certainty	Important or necessary conversations
Steady, unwavering	Vacation, time off (without work tools?)
Ardent	Religious or spiritual practice
Authentic	Neighborhood/community projects
Committed, steadfast, fervent	Play (fun, frolic, reading)
Fervent	Health/Well-being (eating habits, diet, slowing down in life)
Consistent	Errands
Add your own:	Add your own:

Step 1: Pick one aspect of wholehearted from Column A and one activity from Column B.

I will adopt and enter emotion of (Column A) _____
while doing (Column B) _____

Step 2: Envision the result of combining the emotion with the activity.

- Spend some time imagining what life would be like if you succeeded at this combo.

Hint: If you find yourself not quite able to imagine how to go about something from the attitude listed, check out the Insights From Others examples or try another combination.

_____

_____

_____

_____

_____

Step 3: Design a way of fulfilling it to your satisfaction. What is desired result or outcome?

- What will you start and stop doing? How often will you practice and for how long? (Daily for 15 minutes? Or 5 times a day for 2 minutes? Divide into parts?)
- If you honored both A and B, what would you do? Not do? Tend to say? Not want to say anymore?
- What physical characteristics will support you in this implementation? (Breathing pattern, posture, pace of movement, tone of voice, facial expression)
- Use a dictionary or thesaurus if needed to give you synonyms, antonyms, and nuances to increase your understanding and foster ideas.

Step 4: Practice!

Personal Reflections

(What worked? What didn't? What did you adjust?)

_____

_____

_____

_____

_____

_____

_____

_____

_____

_____

INSIGHTS FROM OTHERS

Example:

- I will enthusiastically declutter and organize my garage.

- **End result:** I see myself finally parking my car IN the garage and finding tools and supplies as I need them. I see open and closed shelves and a clean floor.

- **Design:** Labels on the closed storage. All trash, broken tools, and dried paint are tossed. Donate or toss what I haven't used in years. To keep up my enthusiasm, I will work at least 30 minutes and not more than two hours. I can spend $300 for supplies, containers, etc.

◆

I was intrigued by the idea of purposelessness. (How could one NOT be tied to meaning and goals? Was that possible? Was that even an okay way to be? I prided myself in being productive and efficient. Why was I so attracted to being without a purpose or aim?) So I picked Authentic

Purposelessness. My goal was that every day, for a week, I would spend some time without purpose.

The first day I sat down on my couch and watched what happened outside my window. I watched the trees move with the breeze, and the mail delivery. I felt guilty not doing anything. I looked at my watch after what seemed like an hour. Five minutes had passed. On the second day, I decided to go out in the backyard, and before I knew it my critical self had me weeding and tidying up the "mess." Geez, I was failing at purposelessness! The third day I set up my hammock that had been collecting dust in the garage. Ahhhhh ... now that's the trick for purposelessness. Swinging in the breeze and looking up at the trees and sky. I napped and daydreamed. (For the rest of the week I ended up not using a timer and stayed out until I was done. I just seemed to know when I was ready to move back into the day.) What was surely a waste of precious time turned out to be precious time. I felt rejuvenated. My to-do list seemed like a good idea when I approached it from aliveness instead of burden. Who knew one could get soooo much done after relishing doing nothing?!

◆

I decided to do the dishes in earnest. My trick was noticing *as* I was doing—the feel of the soap on my skin, getting the water temperature just right, the sound of the dishes as I stacked them on the drying rack. I tried to keep the pace of being earnest and getting it done without sacrificing getting each dish and glass clean. I honestly think it was faster this way. I spent no time grumbling about doing the dishes. I just did them. My wife thought I was crazy when I asked her if I could do the dishes because I was having fun.

◆

I did this exercise again. If you remember, I said I failed at purposeless when I went out to my garden and started weeding. Well, my garden DID need a cleanup. Wholehearted #2 for me was Ardent Gardening. Hilarious! First of all, you have to have music for that, so I had my iPod with me. Perfection was the name of the game. I slowly and deliberately pruned, mulched, and fertilized. (Classical music was the trick.) What was astounding was that three hours went by and I was not exhausted. I was genuinely pleased not just after ... but along the way. It was the first time my perfectionism didn't push or rush me. It was more like being impeccable, and that takes time and attention.

✦

I assumed wholehearted meant you had to like what you were doing. Carol wasn't kidding when she said this was for procrastinators. I'd been avoiding cleaning my parents' home out for months after my dad died. The timed exercise worked wonders. I could do anything for 20 minutes. I never expanded the time, as others in my group did. For example, my goal was to fill my trunk with trash bags. When it was full, I was out of there whether the time was up or not. What I had been dreading and avoiding was done in two weeks. I truly appreciated the simplicity and lack of drama.

✦

Watch out for change-back behaviors from others. For example, I was practicing (in an exaggerated way) being cheerful on the phone with my son and he said, "You sound like a crazy teacher!" I wondered if I should change back to my old self … NOT!

✦

I had no idea I had been walking around as if I was oppressed. My wholehearted homework was lightness. I notice I am moving out of the role of being the primary bitchy/naggy/grumpy person at home and work. Others around me fill the role and say the kind of thing that I previously would have been the one to say. (Guess I'm not the only "dissatisfaction waiting to happen" person around!)

✦

I notice I'm nicer/more kind/more gentle with myself as well as others.

✦

I am experiencing: giddiness, silliness, happiness, contentment and approaching joy and gratitude … I feel them just around the corner.

✦

Since yesterday, I am practicing wholeheartedly being sick with a cold, allowing myself to rest when I am tired and to be active when I have energy. I practiced satisfaction this morning by *choosing* to keep two client calls this morning rather than cancel, knowing that while I wasn't feeling great, I didn't have to be perfect. I gave myself permission to move forward, without overanalyzing through endless "what-iffing" ahead of time. I set my conditions for satisfaction ahead of time: I would stay on the calls provided I could be present with my clients, and that if I was not able to do that, I would make a request of my client to reschedule when I felt better.

As I finish this, I realize how my story is much different now than it was even six months ago. As I write, I realize other times that I have been practicing satisfaction and wholeheartedness, sometimes without conscious thought. Wow—this emotional agility and emotional competence gets easier with practice. Imagine that—what we practice becomes more natural … I think Carol Courcy might be on to something here ;-).

Author's Story… My wholehearted trick was music. I hated and avoided doing budgets. I have a "shuffle" feature on my music system and put on four CDs of different genres (Rock 'n' roll, classical, country, and New Age). I had no idea which music would come up, and with each new song I wholeheartedly mimicked the rhythm as I filled in my budget figures on the spreadsheet. The music totally distracted me from my normal "I hate this … poor me" attitude.

FREQUENTLY ASKED QUESTIONS

How much practice before you see results and achieve your goals?

It depends. Honestly, I do not mean to be vague.

You will see results as you do each activity. Practicing on a regular basis will exponentially increase your results, awareness, and skill. How much time to spend practicing or how often should you practice? Is once a week enough? Once or twice a day? You will be the judge.

Are *you* satisfied with your progress? If so, keep it up. Find what works for you and do it!

Reaching your ultimate goal is another matter. It depends on many factors: How hard you make it for yourself or others to change is one factor. Undoing an emotion from years and years of practicing usually takes longer to unravel and dispel than an emotion you encounter every once in a while.

Environment is another factor. Those around you and the environment in which you live influence your emotional vitality and agility. If you live in a toxic home or workplace, being ambitious and satisfied requires resiliency and vigilance. Leaving toxic places and relationships and immersing yourself in environments of mutual respect increases the speed of learning the Universal Emotions of Well-being.

> *Author's Story...* It took me several years to change my relationship with my mom. We had a 40-year tradition of being critical of each other and ourselves. We had a lethal combination of both feeling "right" about our own ways and feeling how wrong the other was, and we were bent on fixing the other. She used to say, "Any good daughter would know what I want." She wanted a better daughter. I wanted a better mother. With never enough on both sides, those two twains would never meet.
>
> An outcome of my learning that I was a resentful person was altering how I behaved with my mom. I stopped trying to change her. Openness was my initial goal. When I started practicing it around her, mom was suspicious. At one point, she said, "Don't pull that coaching s—t on

me." (I could always count on my mom's speaking up and her well-honed intuition—dammit!) Truthfully, my initial openness was not that sincere! I was still trying to manipulate her to my ways.) After my initial mistake, I took my practicing elsewhere (work projects and clients) until I felt more competent and sincere and not forcing my shoulds on her.

My emotional learning then took a left-hand turn. Being more open was *not* the emotion that worked to improve my relationship with my mom. It was being more lighthearted and letting up on criticism—giving and getting. Instead of taking each and every one of her critical comments soooooo seriously, I "let them be" more often. I'd always blamed what *she* did for my reaction. I accepted my own skills of guilt and regret. My self-criticism was on par with hers. (I discovered she was harder on herself than on me. WOW ... What a way to live?) I thought we'd both enjoy a vacation from criticism. One day out of my mouth came: "Can we spend less time criticizing _____ (a family member), and more time helping me redecorate my house?" (A talent of hers.) Gradually she shifted as I had. By actively altering my emotion (how I acted around her), *we* actively changed what we talked about. I respected her decorating talents. I avoided old traps by finding ways of being happier with her and her with me. For months, my homework assignment was to make her laugh each time we spoke.

What is a practice?

Simply said, repetition. Perform or do habitually.

> *Luck is the residue of design.* ~ Branch Rickey
> (Former owner of the Brooklyn Dodgers baseball team)

Understanding how our brain operates helps us understand emotional learning activities as a kind of agility training. Repetition fuels learning. Practice builds skill, competence, and confidence. Although this is common sense, this is why practicing emotional agility works:

> The sine qua non (indispensable factor) of a neural network
> is its penchant for strengthening neuronal patterns in
> direct proportion to their use. The more often you do, or

think, or imagine a thing, the more probable it is that your mind will revisit its prior stopping point. [14]

Martha Graham, world-famous dancer and choreographer, offers a more poetic interpretation of practicing in "An Athlete of God":

> I believe that we learn by practice. Whether it means to learn to dance by practicing dancing or to learn to live by practicing living, the principles are the same. In each, it is the performance of a dedicated precise set of acts, physical or intellectual, from which comes shape of achievement, a sense of one's being, a satisfaction of spirit. One becomes, in some area, an athlete of God.
>
> Practice means to perform, over and over again in the face of all obstacles, some act of vision, of faith, of desire. Practice is a means of inviting the perfection desired. [15]

While I am not selling emotional perfection, becoming competent at shifting among emotions is indeed my intention. Emotional agility is not very different from learning skiing, spreadsheet software, or new cell phone features. Emotional agility requires that we practice enough to create a new emotional habit.

- The more you are grateful, the more gratitude you feel and express.
- The more you hate, the more you will hate.
- The more you smile sincerely, the more you will find things to smile about.

Why the easy way at first? Isn't challenging ourselves a good thing?

Yes, if it doesn't lead to self-doubt, exhaustion, and overwhelm. My personal life philosophy of wanting satisfaction and joy is expressed in this book. Choose what works for you. Adjust your life to YOUR liking!

With learning emotional agility, the level of importance or difficulty is not as important as frequency. If you are leaving being grumpy, resigned, or resentful for satisfaction or happiness, do not start with the hardest person or project that is in most dire need of a new strategy! As with my mom, work up to them! Practice with easier tasks. (As my piano teacher said: Practice your scales.) Increase momentum with quantity and quality.

Author's Story... My coaching homework was to be satisfied 20 times a week. As an expert in NGE (Not Good Enough), I could barely make it once a day. My capacity for satisfaction was about 90 seconds and then I felt nauseated. At some point, I recognized that even the 90 seconds was better than never visiting it!

I was ecstatic when I reached 5 minutes, and then 10 minutes.

My family thinks I am being weird. What do I do?

Be aware that you are interrupting the patterns of others too. Remember, you (and the others involved) are used to your current way of interacting. You have developed a pattern that has been or is about to be interrupted. People will expect you to be the way you have been. Others might resist the change at first or may never change along with you.

Author's Story... I changed friends and a company to surround myself with a supportive environment to enhance my lightness learning. I found I was too susceptible to resentment to resist the temptation when around my fellow whiners at work. When around them I'd fall back into my old pattern of blaming others for my problems. I had to actively change who I spent my time with and began to choose people who embodied the lightness I craved. Pretty soon I was unwelcome at the whiners' table at lunch, so that helped too. I found others who were more positive or eager to do something productive about problems and invited them to lunch. (Although this was quite challenging in the beginning for someone who wants to be liked by everyone, I needed to change teams.) As my Mentor Coach Jan asked me, "Do you want to be liked or respected?" I picked respected.

What about mistakes and discovering what doesn't work?

I have not failed. I've just found 10,000 ways
that won't work. ~ Thomas Alva Edison

Be open to learning what does and doesn't work. You are a beginner; mistakes are to be expected. I am recommending emotional agility—not emotional perfection!

- Expect missteps. When we change *our* way of being, it interrupts what is expected by us and by others. *While learning the cha cha or a waltz, stepping on toes is normal.*
- Scale back when needed, change your goal, or persist at a slower pace.
- Get to know all the facets of both the old and new emotion and how you behave with different people, on different days, and in different scenarios. Emotional agility lets you find the right emotion, at the right time, with the right person, for the right purpose.

INSIGHTS FROM A OTHERS

When I began my coaching with Carol, I understood the idea of practicing an emotion I wanted to learn. What was a surprise was her idea of going back and forth between my old way of being and new (and preferred one.)

That wasn't logical for my brain. I wanted to get rid of my bitterness now and FOREVER! I wanted to only practice exiting rage and anger and be happier.

When she suggested going back and forth between anger and happiness, I thought she was waaaaay off target. By spending some time with my anger in an honest way, I discovered I was insincere in a way about happiness. A profound moment came when I saw how attached I was to being right and how justified my anger and bitterness were—especially about how awful *my ex* is, was, and will continue to be. To be honest, I preferred keeping the blaming part so that he'd suffer, while still wanting to be free of my own suffering and be happier.

I soon found that was not possible. So in the beginning I added selective satisfaction to counteract the anger. (Carol said ANY satisfaction trained those neural pathways!) Later on, practicing joy a little bit at a time freed me from both the suffering and blame. Happiness started to occur without all the effort I had expected.

Final Thoughts for Step 3...

Practice enough to get good at the new emotion. Don't try a few times and then say, "Well, that didn't work." (Recognize resignation arising?)

If you have practiced the "old self" for five or ten years, just think of how good you are at that old way of being. How many thousands of hours have you spent practicing? Could you teach others a trick or two of how to stay there if asked? At this stage, you are unlearning as well as learning.

Recalling that *you used to be happy* does not bring happiness. Being happy on a regular basis does. Spending your days in regret and wishing for something different makes you very good at regretting. Practice taking *I should have* and *I should not have* out of your language to have a different future. What you can change is your future, by not creating more *should haves* or *should not haves*. Shifting emotions happens in the present and influences your future.

Living more often in the emotions you prefer may take some time and effort. My goal for Step 3 is sustainability and having more of your daily life touch joy, satisfaction, and wholeheartedness. With your successes, you will build self-trust, self-confidence, and skill, enabling you to head toward more challenging or important goals.

Take some comfort from the tortoise and hare fable ... persistence wins the race.

> *I find that the harder I work the more luck*
> *I seem to have.* ~ Thomas Jefferson

Create some luck for yourself.

Where to from here?

When ready, check out Step 4: Create and Cross New Finish Lines. This is your move toward using your emotional agility for the rest of your life. You will find ways to extend your version of well-being to the relationships and projects of your choosing. The practicing becomes more natural, and extends over months and sometimes years.

STEP 4: CREATE AND CROSS NEW FINISH LINES

As you have seen in Steps 1–3, emotional agility is simple and easy to activate with some attention, intention, and practice. Step 4 opens a possibility for a significant and sustainable life change. I continue to expound on my bias for well-being and crossing our finish lines satisfied and joyful.

Aristotle suggested, earlier in the book, that activating the right emotion, at the right time, to the right degree, with the right person, for the right purpose, may not be so easy. The not-so-easy part can be opting out of patterns. (We often justify why we do what we do. Leaving those justifications can be tricky. You champion a new self by thwarting your old self.)

As the illustration suggests, Step 4 gives you more ideas and practices through which to choose the "paths" you want to stay on. (By "paths" I mean things such as personal and professional relationships, projects, areas of responsibility, job/position, organizations, profession, career path, etc.) Some paths you will choose to opt out of altogether, while in others you will modify your strategy and behaviors, as you did in Steps 1–3.

Carol's Coaching Corner: I recognize that some of us go well beyond tendencies toward self-sacrificing, never-enough overachieving and could be called Platinum Club members. Most club members I've met want relief. They want to replenish their energies and feel valued for the work they do.

As an emeritus member of the club, I urge you to watch out for resisting what is good for you. Our well-honed patterns of overdoing and holding on too tightly to control form a blockade to our desire for rest and replenishment. It is also a blockade to feeling truly satisfied, wholehearted, and joyful. Some of us are driven by guilt, rarely feeling the acknowledgment of our contribution. We continue spinning on the hamster wheel when nothing is ever quite enough and changing is too hard.

I also know that we cannot (and possibly should not) retire from what we care about. Therein lies the conundrum. Can we serve others AND ourselves? Can serving NOT be slavery? Must one always be sacrificed for the other? To some extent, yes and no. I personally believe that these days our communities need a lot of people who care. However, exhausting ourselves for the sake of a cause or belief eventually takes us out of service. We are left with regret and often resentment for how hard we worked and how much we sacrificed. What a waste.

If you are like me and hundreds of other current or emeritus club members I've met, I predict that when leaving some of your longer and stronger patterns, you will resist the rest and replenishment. You will actually resist and have all sorts of good excuses for NOT getting what you say you want.

RESISTANCE IS A GOOD SIGN

When approaching our learning edges—even developing those emotions we deem beneficial—we encounter resistance. Have you wondered why resistance often follows a good or even great idea? Why a couple of weeks after a heartfelt New Year's resolution we have very good reasons why we haven't gotten started? Even when we know in our hearts and minds it is good for us, we experience fear, defiance, or holding back. As high achievers, if we put ourselves onto too many paths with "not enough yet" as our common motivator, we also run the risk of finishing without satisfaction and joy, or not finishing at all. (Remember what you checked off on the "Self-Sacrificing, Never-enough, Overachieving" checklist in the preface? If we persist in those "risky behaviors," we extend the cycle of emotions related to resentment, disappointment, second-guessing and regret.)

Why do we go back to old ways of being, such as procrastination, or emotions that lead us to a standstill, like worry, self-doubt, fretting, and frustration?

Why isn't changing easier?

Welcome to being human! Resistance is natural. In fact it is a GOOD sign! As a way of taking us away from our should and need patterns (*"I should be better/I need to ..."*), let us look carefully at what is surprisingly normal about resistance, fear, and the process of changing. We are being fully human when we automatically go back to old habits and patterns. Why? Homeostasis.

Definition of homeostasis: The natural tendency of a system to move toward its equilibrium or state of balance and away from change.

We naturally move away from change! Any change from our norm takes us off balance. Our automatic reaction when off balance is to regain our balance—even when we do not like our "life as usual" (our current homeostasis). Understanding homeostasis gives us clues as to why we cannot easily change our behavior or maintain changes. Perfect examples are our oldest emotions: Fight, Flight, and Freeze. When change is in the offing or has already started, we aren't choosing our reaction. We find ourselves fighting against something, trying to flee the situation, or feeling or being paralyzed or mute and unable to move or speak.

It is the job of homeostasis to maintain the status quo. Like gravity, it pulls us in the direction of our current life patterns and the array of emotions in our current wardrobe. Resistance is to be expected when changing our well-honed patterns. Once again, we are predictable.

However, when we want to change and learn something, we MUST take ourselves off balance and outside our norm for a period. The good news is that as we learn, we enter a new homeostasis—a new sense of balance. Whether we're learning to play the piano, ski, or wear a new emotion, each time we practice the new, the pull back to the old self lessens. The new self becomes more comfortable. At some point, that ease with the new self becomes the new normal.

Carol's Coaching Corner: Little or no change will happen if we stop ourselves at the first sign of resistance or discomfort. Stopping at that early point will certainly return us to what we have been doing, saying, feeling, and thinking. However, each time we return to an undesirable or destructive pattern, there is a cost to our well-being. Repeated over time, moments of sadness expand to regretting. Repeated disappointment grows into resentment and spreads to other relationships and situations. Ongoing anger becomes bitterness.

As Aristotle said, we are what we repeatedly do. Like any pattern, frequent resistance increases our skill at resisting! Do you want to become more skillful in resistance? Are you resisting and expecting life and others around you to change?

Emotional agility allows us to disrespect our resistance in a healthy way and smooth the path for making changes we enjoy and later appreciate.

The resistance is a signal from your mind and body that a change is in the offing. What is the right amount of resistance for you?

Welcome Resistance!

When resistance arises, look to it as a sign that your current homeostasis (current pattern) is about to change. Watch out for your mind and body's tendency to stay the same. It may begin in earnest with:

Maybe I shouldn't. ✦ *Have I considered how hard it will be?* ✦ *I can't right now.* ✦ *I'm too busy.* ✦ *Maybe tomorrow.* ✦ *It won't make a difference anyway.*

The authors of *A General Theory of Love* use the term "neural attunement" (joining another's emotion) and "mapping the emotional vista" of another for ways of seeking a connection. For example, how hard is it for you to remain happy when surrounded by grumpy people? Or for the opposite, how hard is it to maintain your grumpiness when around happy folks? Stick around happy and fun people and you will feel out of place with your grumpiness. Open yourself to a different emotion, and neural attunement helps you "catch" their happier state.

Or … if you are persistent, they will catch your grumpiness!

AWARENESS ACTIVITY
Which paths are you already on?

This activity shows neural attunement in action. Where and with whom we spend a good amount of time influences *our* emotions.

Emotions at work?

- What would you describe as the variety of emotions of your workplace and the people you work with? What about customers' or vendors' emotions? Your profession? Your industry?

_____

_____

_____

_____

What about your family?

- What emotions do you expect to arise during holidays or special events?
- What emotions do you and certain family members bring to gatherings?
- If and when you do not interact with your family, which emotions arise in you as you consider the possibility of seeing them? After you decide not to?

_____

_____

_____

_____

AWARENESS ACTIVITY

Tune in to the emotions of environments

Take some time and pay attention to what happens to *you* emotionally when you enter places (meetings, conferences, parties, etc.).

- What emotion comes over you as you anticipate arriving? As you enter?
- How might these different emotions influence your day-to-day life and your desires?
- What suits you? What does not?

_____

_____

_____

_____

_____

EMOTIONS ARE CONTAGIOUS

Another reason for having the agility to change emotions is their contagious nature. We can "catch" emotions from others. Have you ever been to a sporting event or concert and been taken by the energy? Have you ever been caught up in an argument not of your making? Have you ever arrived someplace and left in a totally different emotion? (Gone to a comedy club and your "bad mood" disappeared? Been happy until you arrived at a family gathering?) The authors of *A General Theory of Love* help us understand what is happening:

Limbic resonance is the term for emotions being contagious.

> The limbic activity of those around us draws our emotions into almost immediate congruence. That's why a movie viewed in a theater of thrilled fans is electrifying, when its living room version disappoints—it's not the size of the screen or the speakers (as the literal minded home

electronics industry would have it), it's the crowd that releases storytelling magic, the essential, communal, multiplied wonder. The same limbic evocation sends waves of emotion rolling through a throng, making scattered individuals into a unitary, panic-stricken herd or hate-filled lynch mob. [16]

Although limbic resonance and other people's emotions influence the quality of our life, we are not always aware that we fall into emotions due to our environment or the people around us. We find shared emotions in organizations' cultures and family systems. Unless we are very resilient (our own emotion is stronger than the environment), we will catch or fall into the emotions and action patterns of the groups we live, work, play, and socialize with.

Sometimes who we are and what we repeatedly do is activated by those we spend time with.

Carol's Coaching Corner: Notice I use terms like *activate*, *catch*, or *fall into*, when I speak about emotions as contagious. I do not use *caused by* or *because of.* This is intentional on my part.

Many of us speak as if circumstances, people, or situations cause our reactions. *They/he/she/it made me. I had no choice. It's their fault I am unhappy. If it weren't for them* ... Although there are elements of truth to these statements, the problem I have with causality is that we cannot easily change others—especially when they do not want to or elect to change.

Our lives can improve dramatically when we change ourselves. Hopefully in Steps 1–3 you have already seen how much you can change your own life experience by interrupting patterns and creating new ones. Others may or may not join you. That is why you will eventually opt out of some paths you are on.

I do not want you to pin your hopes on others behaving differently BEFORE you do something different. You could be waiting for a long, long time.

PERSONAL WORKSHEET

What emotions do you catch?

In this activity you will speculate on how others' emotions influence you. What emotions are you exposed to, and which of these do you tend to catch? Also a part of this activity is assessing your level of satisfaction with your current situation.

Carol's Coaching Corner: In case you find yourself falling into anxiety, anger, or spending more time thinking about other people and what they do or don't do, this is an awareness activity for you to recognize the emotions YOU catch! Activate a more neutral emotion by changing your breathing pattern and get back to the activity.

Name of individual or group: _____

Emotion you would say they spend their time in:

_____

_____

_____

What emotion do *you* "catch"? What is your reaction? (How does their emotion or attitude influence your life, your goals, and relationships?)

_____

_____

_____

What is your level of satisfaction?

_____

_____

_____

Anything to alter or leave behind?

_____

_____

_____

Name of individual or group: _____

Emotion you would say they spend their time in:

_____

_____

_____

What emotion do _you_ "catch"? What is your reaction? (How does their emotion or attitude influence your life, your goals, and relationships?)

_____

_____

_____

What is your level of satisfaction?

_____

_____

_____

Anything to alter or leave behind?

_____

_____

_____

Name of individual or group: _____

Emotion you would say they spend their time in:

_____

_____

_____

What emotion do _you_ "catch"? What is your reaction? (How does their emotion or attitude influence your life, your goals, and relationships?)

_____

_____

_____

What is your level of satisfaction?

_____

_____

_____

Anything to alter or leave behind?

_____

_____

_____

PERSONAL WORKSHEET
Which paths to stay on

Directions: Given your reflections from the Personal Worksheets on prior pages, what will you do to be more satisfied?

Which paths will you continue?

_____

_____

_____

_____

_____

Which paths will you leave behind or spend less time on?

_____

_____

_____

_____

_____

Where will you adjust your emotional agility for increased satisfaction? What emotions will you activate and practice in each situation to sustain satisfaction?

_____

_____

_____

_____

_____

Carol's Coaching Corner: What if we encounter resistance from others?

First of all, I can almost guarantee you *will* to some extent experience resistance from others. You have your emotional patterns and level of emotional agility. They have theirs. Sometimes the people or environments we are a part of are not looking to change. Family systems and organizational cultures are often good examples. We get our hopes up with passionate desires for making things better and often think or a-s-s-u-m-e change is needed and wanted by others. (*After all, I am right. I know better.*)

ALERT! When you encounter resistance over and over, it can put all your ambitions, good advice, and right decisions on the defensive or in decline. When we find resistance from others, we have some options: 1) We change ourselves. Via emotional agility we can adjust our emotions and behavior, thereby changing our expectations of what will and will not happen. We directly influence our level of satisfaction. However, that does not guarantee others will change to our liking. 2) We can also adjust how often we interact with others, an environment, or family system.

One of my favorite quotes: "The definition of insanity is doing the same thing over and over again, expecting different results."-Rita Mae Brown

Change yourself. Change what you can change. Your changing will affect others. And if they resist, so be it. You have the choice to go back or go forward. Emotional agility requires willing players. Find and surround yourself with willing players.

INSIGHTS FROM OTHERS

Even though I truly want to leave my self-sacrificing ways, I was awash with resistance from these few questions. All of a sudden my personal wellness was my job in life. It felt like I'd gained weight. My instinct was to go back and practice more, but my super-achiever tendency says going back is shameful and embarrassing. Thankfully I honored my instinct and went back to Step 3 for a while to shore up my satisfaction.

◆

DUH! You mean I don't have to hang around "them"? How simple is it to spend less time around my complaining family members? I can't abandon them, but I can leave the room.

◆

While doing the "Which paths to continue?" it suddenly dawned on me that like a crusader I am choosing to champion my causes at work. But there is no budget for my "great ideas." My pushing them on my bosses every chance I get creates frustration in me and irritates them. Rita May Brown is right. I am crazy if I keep doing more of the same.

◆

I was able to get off my high horse of righteousness with my sister. You asked in class whether we wanted to be right or happy. For a decade I chose being right. This chapter opened a possibly of letting go of something that happened when we were in college. It's been long enough.

IMMERSION: EXTENDING EMOTIONS INTO MOODS

Although we have been isolating emotions for learning purposes, we live day-to-day life within a mixture of emotions. We wake up in an emotion, whether familiar or unfamiliar. Depending on what happens during the day, we feel shifts. Some emotions we characterize as constructive while others we say are detrimental. In one day or a week, it can feel like gentle ups and downs or like a roller coaster ride.

Our aim through the learning and activities in this book is to cross finish lines satisfied and joyful. So what do we do with all these ups and downs? In terms of emotional agility, immersion in an emotion allows us to influence our overall mood or attitude toward life.

Carol's Coaching Corner: The more time you spend in an emotion, the easier it is to access. Over time and with practice, it becomes a part of your "norm." I call this your "home mood." You will continue to have some ups and downs; however, it is easier and faster to return to your norm. Another common experience reported by clients is that they tend to worry much less about their detrimental emotions. They trust that "this too shall pass." If you want an emotion to pass faster, all your emotional agility skills so far will help you.

At some point you may want to smooth out your ups and downs (commonly achieved by learning satisfaction and contentment). At other times you may want to increase the ups and downs (commonly achieved by learning excitement and joy).

In the upcoming activities, you will extend the time you spend in emotions associated with satisfaction and joy. The goal is that they hang around longer and that you get a real sense whether you like and want more of them.

Immersion into Gratitude

In my learning circles, gratitude journals are a very popular activity.[17] And for some this idea of being grateful is brand-new. What I offer here is connecting being grateful with the idea of increasing our susceptibility to emotions that bring us satisfaction and joy. (Remember the health benefits of gratitude from page 98?) This immersion exercise builds on the notion of you creating some emotional compound interest so that satisfaction and joy will be frequent emotional visitors.

SIMPLE PRACTICE
Thank others game

One and only rule: Say some form of "thank you" *20 times a day for a week.*

The language of gratitude:

I appreciate …   I am grateful for …   I honor …

I recognize you for …   Thank you!

I thank you for …   In gratitude …   I praise …

To win at this game you must speak the language of gratitude. It will not work unless you are sincere. For example:

- Whether on the phone or in person, as you complete a transaction, thank the sales person. (Grocery store, gas station, post office.)
- Find reasons to thank employees, contractors, bosses, clerks, vendors, colleagues.
- Offer some version of gratitude somewhere in each email.
- Write a thank-you note or email.
- Send an electronic "thank you" greeting card.
- Contact someone you have not thanked yet, and thank them.
- Find opportunities to thank or praise others during and at the end of a meeting.
- ANY time someone gives you something, no matter how minor, simple, insignificant, trivial, or LATE—say "Thank you!"

Carol's Coaching Corner: You are building your neural pathways of gratitude and appreciation. Repetition is more important than significance at this point. In this case more frequency is indeed better than more effort.

For optimal benefits, mean it when you say it.

Personal Reflections

What happened for you?

_____

_____

_____

_____

What did you notice about others?

_____

_____

_____

_____

INSIGHTS FROM OTHERS

To my surprise, the *Thank Others Game* was difficult at first. I had no idea how ungrateful I'd become about those around me.

◆

Twenty times a day? Are you kidding? It took me a week to get my first 20. I discovered how isolated I was. I was not interacting with people. I had to get out there in life to do this practice.

◆

At first I felt very little benefit to me. No wholehearted gratitude coming from me was my insight. I reread the instructions and there it was … sincerity. Unless I looked people in the eyes or actually paid attention to what I was saying or writing in the email, I did not feel the benefit.

◆

I discovered I hold grudges. Even when there was a good reason to thank one of my employees, I couldn't bring myself to thank him because of a mistake he made earlier this year that made me look bad. Since then, he has been trying to make up for it by doing really good work. I hadn't moved on! I thank you and I am pretty sure he would thank you for inventing this exercise.

SIMPLE PRACTICE
Appreciation games

These two activities are specifically for active members of the Self-sacrificing, Never-enough, Overachieving Club who are currently suffering from self-criticism, self-blame, and/or self-disappointment.

Remember the phrase "We are what we practice"? Compound emotional interest works with negative and destructive emotions as well as positive ones. Be mindful of what you are putting into motion each day.

I chose the title "games" to activate a bit of our natural achiever's competitiveness. This time you are competing for personal benefit.

Will you make it a win-win?

Carol's Coaching Corner: Whether you feel like it or not, DO these gratitude activities. Whether or not you think there is much to be grateful for, take this opportunity to excite your brain with something other than negativity!

You do not have to wait to be motivated. Motivation will arrive after you begin.

Appreciation Game 1:

Write a list of 50 things or people you are grateful to or for.

1	26
2	27
3	28
4	29
5	30
6	31
7	32
8	33
9	34
10	35
11	36
12	37
13	38
14	39
15	40
16	41
17	42
18	43
19	44
20	45
21	46
22	47
23	48
24	49
25	50

Personal Reflections

_____

_____

_____

_____

_____

_____

Appreciation Game 2:

Write a list of 25 things about yourself that you appreciate or are thankful for.

1	
2	
3	
4	
5	
6	
7	
8	
9	
10	
11	
12	
13	
14	
15	
16	
17	
18	
19	
20	
21	
22	
23	
24	
25	

Personal Reflections

_____

_____

_____

_____

_____

_____

INSIGHTS FROM OTHERS

It took me over a month to list the 50 things to be grateful for. On the way there I could have written a list of 1,000 things or people I was angry at and disappointed in. This revelation has been uncomfortable, to say the least. How did I get so far down the path of bitterness? I have a grumpy attitude almost everywhere. And then I remembered your story of discovering being resentful. Bitterness is an opening for me too. Odd that a feeling of calm is a part of this too. Thank you. (See … I remembered the exercise!)

✦

I was grateful for the blue sky, my dog, my tomato plants, my new set of pots and pans. To get to 50 I had to really stretch. (A lint-free dryer, finding my keys, staples in my stapler, no bills in the mail today.)

As I reread my list of 50 things, I noticed not *one* of them was anything about me personally. It had not even occurred to me. I was struck by how poorly I held myself. Nothing to esteem there. And then I noticed #2.

I wanted to skip the second one. Why bother after the game 1 insight? Thank you, by the way, for only having us write 25 good things about ourselves. Even that took some time. Somehow, I think you designed this exercise with me in mind.

✦

When I first saw the second activity, I heard an authority voice in my head saying, "There you go again, being self-absorbed. You shouldn't do for yourself EVER." Screaming in my head was "A good person ONLY does for others." As you suggested, I did Game 2 anyway. So I had to start doing things for myself so I could be thankful and do my homework!

I also continued doing for others with more sincerity and without strings attached. The difference? I was doing it out of generosity and not guilt. What a sense of freedom. THANK YOU. ☺

✦

Dear Carol,

Thank you for the wonderful quarterly call on emotional agility and gratitude. It was a powerful call, and I've been thinking about it ever since. I am familiar with gratitude and the benefits of a journal, so I am choosing altruism/generosity—which I haven't consciously practiced as much. They are outward focused and seem to move me quicker into an emotional shift to joy and satisfaction.

✦

If I think this through in my usual perfectionist style, I'll worry this email to death and never send it ... Here goes ...

Gratitude has been the big antidote for the mood of resignation I've been going in and out of for several weeks now. I've been practicing acknowledgment of the people who won't listen to me or believe in me so much that I disbelieve myself. My practice is focusing on all the blessings of my life ... and as I bathe in the love and support of those around me, my heart lightens and a smile, twinkle in my eye, and flutter of joy start to emerge. I offer this up with love, gratitude, appreciation, and today, a playful instead of resigned spirit.

SIMPLE PRACTICE
Personal gratitude breaks

Want more joy in life? A deeper sense of well-being? Less fear and anxiety? In addition to a coffee break, take a "gratitude break" each day as a path to joy:

- Every day for a week, sometime during the day, stop what you are doing and take a five-minute break to appreciate life. Say some version of *"Thank You, Life!"*
- Statements like these do *not* require reasons. Your life does not have to change one iota for you to say "Thank you" to life. Declaring it and meaning it is enough for the body and mind to activate and recover the emotion of joy. Bit by bit, you will also feel it.

Carol's Coaching Corner: If you have difficulty activating gratitude for life, repeat this earlier activity: Stand up, face a window with a view or a lovely piece of art, even a plant, and open your arms up and out. Palms open and up as if to receive. Lift your eyes up and look outward. Let the feeling or energy of gratitude coming to you wash over you. (It may take a bit of time. Take the time you need to get hints and hits of joy.) THANK YOU, LIFE!

Bonus Practice: Like what you get? Do this daily for a month, a quarter, or a year!

Personal Reflections

What would you say has been your "compound interest" from these gratitude activities?

_____

_____

_____

_____

_____

_____

_____

_____

_____

_____

Lessons learned about lightness from dogs

This list is all over the Internet. Although I could not find the original source, I am grateful for the author's humor and delightful insights:

If a dog were the teacher, you would learn stuff like:

- When loved ones come home, always run to greet them.
- Never pass up the opportunity to go for a joyride.
- Allow the experience of fresh air and the wind in your face to be pure ecstasy.
- When it is in your best interest, practice obedience.
- Let others know when they have invaded your territory.
- Take naps.
- Stretch before rising. (Is that where they got the downward dog yoga pose?)
- Run, romp and play daily.
- Thrive on attention and let people touch you.

- Avoid biting when a simple growl will do.
- On warm days, stop to lie on your back on the grass.
- On hot days, drink lots of water and lie under a shady tree.
- When you are happy, dance around and wag your entire body.
- No matter how often you are scolded, do not pout or buy into the guilt thing. Run right back and make friends.
- Delight in the simple joy of a long walk.
- Eat with gusto and enthusiasm. Stop when you have had enough.
- Be loyal.
- Never pretend to be something you are not.
- When someone is having a bad day, be silent, sit close by, and nuzzle them gently.

SIMPLE PRACTICE

Ten-weeks of lightness

▬▬▬▬▬▬▬▬▬▬▬

Pick any 10 of these "lessons from dogs."

Week 1:
Week 2:
Week 3:
Week 4:
Week 5:
Week 6:
Week 7:
Week 8:
Week 9:
Week 10:

Each week, for ten weeks in a row, honor the intent of one practice. All week long, be mindful to adjust your thinking and behavior to mimic the spirit of the phrase you are practicing.

- How will you remind yourself?
- Review the INSIGHTS FROM OTHERS that follow for ideas if needed.

Personal Reflections

- What happened for you?
- Were you able to feel a sense of lightness?
- What did you notice about the reactions of others?
- What will you keep doing or change for the future?

_____

_____

_____

_____

INSIGHTS FROM OTHERS

It never occurred to me to enjoy my walks. Exercise, not enjoyment, was my goal before this activity. My dog ALWAYS enjoys our walks. He can't wait. He grabs the leash and waits by the door. I "copied" his energy, and lo and behold, it WAS fun.

✦

I guess I should have known by now that your exercises are not trivial. Initially I thought of skipping this one. (After all, I am a serious person and this is stupid—to be taking advice from dogs.) My wife mentioned how grumpy I'd been with the kids lately, so I picked romping and playing. Every night after dinner we played. I did a horrible job at leading play. Too structured. The kids said it wasn't fun at all and asked their mom if they could play video games instead. Bless my wife, who suggested I let the kids choose what we'd do. Although horrified at first (they made up all sorts of crazy rules), I just kept breathing to allow them to be in charge. We really did have fun. We wrestled—a no-no in our house—until we were exhausted from laughing and playing. I am back to enjoying being a dad.

✦

As soon as I read "let people touch you," tears welled up in my eyes. I took that as a sign of some sort. No one touched me. I had to go first. So I started hugging my family. With strangers I "hugged" them with my eyes or when I thanked them. I got a few strange looks and averted eyes, so I scaled back a bit and just acknowledged their presence. I feel more touched and tenderness seems more than okay. My daughter even hugged me first.

✦

Obedience? Are you kidding? I didn't even see the words "when in your best interest" when I read this the first time. (I remembered what you said about emotional reverberation ... that we see what the emotion we are in allows us to see. I'd call it cognitive blindness.) I found I confused obedience with punishment and feeling oppressed or forced. At work I was known (with pride) as the resident cynic. I took a shot at seeing if this lightness idea really works. I stopped criticizing anything and everything in the coffee room. I started doing what people asked without a scowl on my face. One colleague asked if I was sick. It took awhile, but this lightness stuff isn't so bad after all. People have started asking my opinion. Except for the negative break room crew, that had never happened to me before.

SIMPLE PRACTICE
The ABCs of your life

You can find inspiration in all sorts of places. Case in point? A needlepoint on a friend's office wall inspired this activity. [18]

In the spirit of cultivating and honoring our intentions toward crossing finish lines, what are the satisfied and joyful ABCs of *your* life you wish to demonstrate to yourself? Others?

Directions:

1. Review the "ABCs of Life" in the left column on page 184. Are there any qualities or attitudes you aspire to that point you in the direction of satisfaction or joy? What others come to mind?

2. In the right column, revise the list to reflect YOUR ABCs.

   - Change the phrases to suit your personal aspirations and values.

   - The recommendation is that you choose something that guides you toward well-being. However, what you choose is totally up to you.

3. You will be living EACH of the 26 qualities for a selected period of time. (One a day. One a week. One a month. As you choose.)

   - For example, if you pick "daily," you will do your ABCs one day at a time, over a period of 26 days. (Day 1 = A, Day 2 = B, etc.)

   - "Weekly" is once a week over 26 weeks. (Week 1 = A, Week 2 = B, etc.)

4. Whatever time period you choose, shape your life (what you say and do) to reflect the qualities you selected.

Carol's Coaching Corner: Again, I am promoting emotional agility ... not emotional perfection. What would be a satisfying improvement?

ABCs of Life	YOUR ABCs of Life
Accept differences.	A
Be kind.	B
Count your blessings.	C
Dream.	D
Express thanks.	E
Forgive.	F
Give freely.	G
Harm no one.	H
Imagine more.	I
Jettison anger.	J
Keep confidences.	K
Love truly.	L
Master something.	M
Nurture hope.	N
Open your mind.	O
Pack lightly.	P
Quell rumors.	Q
Reciprocate.	R
Seek wisdom.	S
Touch hearts.	T
Understand.	U
Value truth.	V
Win graciously.	W
Xeriscape.	X
Yearn for peace.	Y
Zealously support a worthy cause.	Z

INSIGHTS FROM OTHERS

I found myself a bit overwhelmed with such a long assignment. I guess well-being and I haven't been friends much these days. So to relieve some pressure to "do it right and well," I decided to adopt the list as is and do one a day.

There were several I didn't quite get. (Like Xeriscape.) I don't have a garden. I heard myself say, "I should have a garden." Sheesh, I am consistently never good enough. But then since this was a well-being exercise, I decided that no garden is the ultimate Xeriscape! Another one was "touch hearts." When I read it, MY heart was touched. I decided I didn't have to go any further with that one either. My favorite was "count your blessings." I simply reread my gratitude lists.

This was a wonderful lesson for me in doing what was asked, following the instructions to make it work for me, without always pushing for more and shoulding myself so I always come up short. My impatience with never ever measuring up is growing! (I imagine you smiling, Carol.)

✦

I changed all of them. That in itself was a lesson in choosing what I say I value and who I am in the world. So I focused ALL letters on a big project at work that is due in seven months. 'A' became Advance the PPO project. B is Below Budget. C is find Champions. X became eXpect success (e was already taken).

I took some liberties for c and x. But since I am in charge of my satisfaction on this one, I get to create it my way. LOVE that part. I posted this on my white board for all to see. I've even had some people offer to help me with a letter. In the end we didn't do it weekly. Instead the whole list became the reminder of how we wanted to fulfill on this project. (We were early AND under budget in delivering the PPO and had some laughs on the way.)

✦

Honestly, at this low point in my life, this was too much for me. So I just did "open my mind" for the last month. That was plenty for a glimpse of satisfaction. Joy is a bit too much for me to believe in at this point. My resignation has been fully fired for some time and simply being open was a big stretch for me. I notice I am less tired. Not sure that's related. Is it?

Carol's Coaching Corner: The strategy behind these exercises is personal creativity as your skill in making desirable changes via emotional agility increases. I modeled the exercises after my experiences, and continue to be fascinated by how creative and insightful my students and clients are about their own journeys. I welcome hearing what *you* discover and invent.

www.saveyourinnertortoise.com

AFTERWORD

WHERE TO FROM HERE?

If you have taken this journey with me to this point, I offer my heartfelt CONGRATULATIONS! Honestly, it took me being brave to get this far, and I suspect you also needed certain amounts of bravery to go against your old commonsense patterns. BRAVO!

I truly hope it was worth the time.

"Where to from here?" is always the question at the end of my teleclass series, workshops, and coaching relationships. Here are my thoughts, given what my students, clients, and I have designed for ourselves:

Use it or lose it. This is a consensus of most all of us who have embarked on this emotional agility journey. The other day one of my former students said, "I totally forgot about wonder." (Her learning goal during her teleclass series.) That reminded me that life has a way of taking over and going back to our old ways without some intention and attention to our emotional agility desires and goals. Homeostasis is a strong pull back to our old self. Who we spend time with also influences our emotions. Intentional practice is required until the desired emotions are embodied—they become natural and readily available.

> *Author's Story...* These days I have an annual emotional learning goal. Over the period of a year, I immerse myself in and play with various activities that foster my chosen emotion. For example, I picked "self-care" back in 2007. Turns out I needed two years for that one.

I had no clue what self-care was. In the first year I was bombarded by *this is selfish and self-absorbed*. (All I was doing was adjusting my work schedule down to 40 hours per week. Sigh! Some old belief patterns die hard in me.) 2009 was determination and focus. Instead of dabbling with writing this book, I committed to finishing it. 2010 was gratitude for dear friends, clients, and colleagues supporting me in fulfilling my dream.

2011 was back to determination and enjoyment. I wanted to enjoy getting this book in your hands and off my to-do list by my 64th birthday. Asking for help, trusting myself, trusting others to help me, laughing and regular bouts with *Who am I kidding?* have been a part of this year. I have had to say no to projects and coaching requests that challenged my "scarcity thinking." (You HAVE to say yes in bad economic times.) However, when I look at my bank balance, I am satisfied. With ever-increasing amounts of satisfaction, contentment is a new emotion for me. It is not as I expected at all. I thought if I was contented, I would not do much of anything. Actually the opposite is true. I don't do EVERYTHING; I do SOME THINGS. Big difference for me.

After all this time—my learning started in the early 1990s—I am profoundly grateful for the idea of emotional agility. In completing this book I have fulfilled a longtime dream. To my delight, I only visit my nemesis of resentment and self-doubt from time to time. I respect them and even my second-guessing as entry points for better decisions. I trust myself to a much greater degree. I have also increased my trust of others. Remember my "itty bitty bitchy committee"? As it turns out, they have my best interests in mind. When I respect them by honestly listening, they raise their voices to make a point instead of ranting and raving. Whew!

When you get stuck, find support. Sometimes we are absolutely the wrong person for ourselves to depend on for changing and getting what we want. Without outside supporters you can trust and be yourself with, your own version of an "itty bitty bitchy committee" will have their way with you. The cost? You will remain right and righteous about what is not working in your life.

Do you want to be right or happy? Going it alone may not be the best strategy. Here are some ideas for moving forward:

- Go back and do the activities and exercises again. **You are not the same human being you were when you first did them.** Use the book like an owner's manual. Flip through the chapters to find what suits you or what you need at the time.
- Do the whole book or some of the simple practices with a group over time.
- Join my blog or take advantage of the FREE stuff on my website: www.saveyourinnertortoise.com
- Join me and fellow learners for a teleclass series live or via a recording, or contact me to discuss one-on-one or group coaching.

And finally...

The following is from one of those inspirational email chain letters that I get every week. I think it is a wonderful example of our goals for this book ... satisfaction and joy. It was supposedly written by an 83-year-old. (I did not find a source or discover if it is true. I frankly do not care. The wisdom is priceless.)

Dear Bertha,

I'm reading more and dusting less.

I'm sitting in the yard and admiring the view without fussing.

About the weeds in the garden ... I'm spending more time with my family and friends and less time working.

Whenever possible, life should be a pattern of experiences to savor, not to endure. I'm trying to recognize these moments now and cherish them.

I'm not "saving" anything; we use our good china and crystal for every special event, such as losing a pound, getting the sink unstopped, or the first Amaryllis blossom.

I wear my good blazer to the market. My theory is if I look prosperous, I can shell out $28.49 for one small bag of groceries.

I'm not saving my good perfume for special parties, but wearing it for clerks in the hardware store and tellers at the bank.

"Someday" and "one of these days" are losing their grip on my vocabulary; if it's worth seeing or hearing or doing, I want to see and hear and do it now.

I'm not sure what others would've done had they known they wouldn't be here for the tomorrow that we all take for granted. I think they would have called family members and a few close friends. They might have called a few former friends to apologize and mend fences for past squabbles. I like to think they would have gone out for a Chinese dinner or for whatever their favorite food was. I'm guessing; I'll never know.

It's those little things left undone that would make me angry if I knew my hours were limited.

Angry because I hadn't written certain letters that I intended to write one of these days.

Angry and sorry that I didn't tell my husband and parents often enough how much I truly love them.

I'm trying very hard not to put off, hold back, or save anything that would add laughter and luster to our lives.

And every morning when I open my eyes, I tell myself that it is special. Every day, every minute, every breath truly is a gift from God.

Thank you for your trust in me, emotional agility, and most of all in yourself, to *Save Your Inner Tortoise!*

ACTIVITY AND SIMPLE PRACTICE INDEX

STEP 2

STEP 3

STEP 4

ACKNOWLEDGMENTS

Writing a book about learning emotional agility was full of ups and downs
—a roller coaster ride of thrills and chills for several years.
I am profoundly grateful for my faithful and skilled supporters.

To my students and clients
for their trust and courage on their paths to emotional agility.

To my weekly mastermind buddies Barb Eisele and Judy Katz
for their wisdom, undying confidence, and honesty.

To my writing coach Judy Duenow
for opening me to the world of writing and having written.

To my teachers Julio Olalla and Fernando Flores
who launched my passion for learning and coaching.

To my brand consultant Emily Aiken
who keeps my brand promise on track.

To my book launch team Beth Kelly, Jessica Epstein, and Frank Steele
whose expertise astounded me.

To my illustrator Giampaolo Bonetti
whose adorable tortoises kept the book light.

And finally…
To my mom, Regina Cram, who despite our rocky road was one of my
best teachers on the road to emotional agility.

To my dad, Wilford Cram, for teaching me lightness of spirit.

NOTES

Good to Know Before You Begin

1. Paul Ekman, PhD, *Emotions Revealed* (Macmillan, 2007), xvii.

2. Thomas Lewis, Fari Amini and Richard Lannon, *A General Theory of Love* (Random House Digital, 2001), 36.

3. *Destructive Emotions: How Can We Overcome Them? A Scientific Dialogue with the Dalai Lama, Narrated by Daniel Goleman* (Bantam Books, 2003).

4. Julia Cameron, *The Sound of Paper* (Penguin, 2005).

5. Aristotle, *The Nichomachean Ethics,* as cited in *Emotional Intelligence,* by Daniel Goleman (Bantam, 10th Anniversary edition, 2006), xix.

Step 2: Give Your Self-sacrificing, Never-enough, Overachieving Tortoise a Break

6. "Universality of Emotion" by Paul Ekman, PhD, in *Destructive Emotions* with the Dalai Lama and Daniel Goleman, 119.

7. Lewis, Amini and Lannon, *A General Theory of Love,* 130.

Step 3: Save Your Inner Tortoise ... Cross Finish Lines Joyful and Satisfied

8. *www.heartmath.org*, The Science of Thanksgiving Gratitude

9. Matthieu Ricard, PhD, *Destructive Emotions*, 72–86.

10. Gabrielle Leblanc, *Five Things Happy People Do*, *http://www. oprah.com/article/omagazine/omag_200803_happy*

11. Rick Hanson, PhD, *Seven Facts About the Brain That Incline the Mind to Joy*, 2007, *www.WiseBrain.org*.

12. David Whyte, *Where Many Rivers Meet* (Many Rivers Press, 1990). Printed with permission from Many Rivers Press.

13. David Whyte, *Crossing the Unknown Sea* (Riverhead Trade, 2002), 132–134.

14. Lewis, Amini and Lannon, *A General Theory of Love*, 143–144.

15. Martha Graham, *An Athlete of God,* essay on National Public Radio, *www.NPR.org*

Step 4: Create and Cross New Finish Lines

16. Lewis, Amini and Lannon, *A General Theory of Love*, 64.

17. Good samples of gratitude practices are available via www. heartmath.org.

18. ABCs of Life—After researching this on Google, I could not acknowledge the original author for their insight. Whoever you are, THANK YOU!

Printed in the United States
by Baker & Taylor Publisher Services